Anonymous

Papers Presented at the Educational Convention of the Congregational Churches

of Southern California. Held at Los Angeles, April 13-14, 1892

Anonymous

Papers Presented at the Educational Convention of the Congregational Churches
of Southern California. Held at Los Angeles, April 13-14, 1892

ISBN/EAN: 9783337165055

Printed in Europe, USA, Canada, Australia, Japan

Cover: Foto ©Lupo / pixelio.de

More available books at **www.hansebooks.com**

PAPERS PRESENTED

AT THE

EDUCATIONAL CONVENTION

OF THE

Congregational Churches

OF

SOUTHERN CALIFORNIA

HELD AT

Los Angeles, April 13-14, 1892.

EVENING EXPRESS COMPANY, PRINTERS,
1892.

PREFACE.

The Executive Committee of the Board of Trustees of Pomona College called an Educational Convention of the Congregational Churches of Southern California to meet in Los Angeles, April 13 and 14, 1892. Representatives of the Churches were present from Santa Barbara, Ventura, Santa Paula, Saticoy, National City, San Diego, Santa Ana, Orange, Riverside, Redlands, San Bernardino, Mentone, Highlands, Rialto, Ontario, Pomona, Claremont, Monrovia, Sierra Madre, Pasadena, South Riverside, Eagle Rock, Long Beach, Vernondale, Oceanside, Escondido, Hyde Park, and the nine Churches of Los Angeles. There were thirty papers upon the program, which opened Wednesday evening, April 13th, at 7:30. Four were absent, and their papers were not read. There were sessions during ten hours, and there was no time for discussion.

The object of the Convention was to confer together thus early in the history of the College, that the best ideas of the constituency might reach the ears of the Board of Trustees who were nearly all present at this meeting. Each speaker had been asked what one idea he would like to emphasize before the Convention and from the themes thus chosen, the following program was then constructed by the Committee, and by vote of the Convention the papers have been edited by the Committee and are printed herewith:

PROGRAM.

I. The Christian College.

	PAGE
REV. W. C. MERRILL, San Diego—The Psychological Necessity for the Christian College	7
REV. J. K. McLEAN, D. D., Oakland—The Building of a Christian College	15
REV. C. G. BALDWIN, President of Pomona College—The Christian College We are Undertaking to Build	26

II. The Christian Element in Education.

REV. H. T. STAATS, Pasadena—Why a Distinctively Christian Education	30
REV. E. R. BRAINERD, San Bernardino—The Imperative Need of Christian Schools	33
REV. E. D. WEAGE, National City—Christian Education and Character Building	39

III. The Student Constituency of a Christian College.

PROF. E. C. NORTON, Pomona College, Claremont—The Student Material for College Building	42
REV. L. H. FRARY, Pomona—Duty of the Church to the Intellectual Life of Her Children	46
REV. C. T. WEITZEL, Santa Barbara—The Personal Factor in Education	50

IV. The Bible and Christian Education.

REV. F. N. MERRIAM, Ventura—The Bible in the Curriculum of the Christian College	57
PROF. C. B. SUMNER, Pomona College, Claremont—The Revival of Bible Study	62

V. The Financiering of a Christian College.

REV. A. E. TRACY, Ontario—The Necessity of Promoting Christian Education by Private Benevolence—Not a Disadvantage	69

VI. Our Community, Our Churches, and Our College.

REV. J. H. HARWOOD, D. D., Orange—The Relation of Christian Education to the Church (manuscript not furnished).

REV. T. C. HUNT, Riverside—Peculiar Conditions in Southern California which make Special Demands upon Pomona College... 73

VII. Single Thoughts on Christian Education.

REV. THOMAS HENDRY, Los Angeles, Park Church—A Plea for Education—Practical and Christian............................ 79

REV. J. H. COLLINS, Los Angeles, Third Church—The Curse of an Education which is not Practical 83

REV. O. D. CRAWFORD, Oceanside—Our Stewardship of the Mind.. 85

PROF. F. W. PHELPS, Washburn College, Kansas—College Extension.. 88

REV. GEO. A. RAWSON, Vernondale—Importance of a Religious Atmosphere.. 93

REV. Henry W. JONES, Escondido—The Workman His Own Best Tool.. 96

REV. STEPHEN BOWERS, Ventura—Christian Education.......... 105

PROF. A. D. BISSELL, formerly Professor of Music in Oahu College, H. I.—Christian Education and Music............... 110

REV. FRANCIS M. PRICE, Los Angeles, Bethlehem—The Transforming Power of College Life............................ 114

VIII. The Open Hour.

Voluntary Addresses. Opportunity for the widest variety of suggestion, each speaker limited to five minutes.

IX. Christian Education and the World's Work.

PROF. C. S. NASH, Pacific Theological Seminary, Oakland—The Kind of Men Demanded by God from the Christian College... 118

REV. ROBERT G. HUTCHINS, Los Angeles, First Church—The Christian College and Our National Perils (manuscript not furnished).

X. Platform of the Educational Convention.

A Series of Resolutions, embodying the practical recommendations of the Convention, prepared by Rev. J. T. Ford and Rev. C. G. Baldwin 126

PAPERS PRESENTED
AT THE
EDUCATIONAL CONVENTION
OF THE
CONGREGATIONAL CHURCHES
OF
SOUTHERN CALIFORNIA.

THE PSYCHOLOGICAL NEED OF A CHRISTIAN EDUCATION.

Rev. W. C. Merrill, San Diego.

It is a fact worthy of note that ignorance is not the parent of a vast sum of the crime that disgraces our land today. Our criminals, thousands of them, are educated criminals. There is a great want somewhere that has not been met in the making of citizens. Men are not seeking legitimate means to attain their ends. They are trying to make stones into bread, forgetting that it was Satan who first offered the bright suggestion. The husbandman who sells small, green, berries by a few fine ones at the top; the grocer who palms off white dirt for sugar and forgets that grit always tells in the end; the dairyman who thinks his "artesian cow" is a great saving of shorts and alfalfa; the merchant who imagines that marking American goods French is the best way to solve the tariff problem and diminish the surplus; the manufacturer who trusts that ground rags and cotton will not tell tales farther on—what shall I say of these men?

Pessimism aside, this is a very considerable product of the education of today. If education do not produce it, it does not prevent it. It does not seem to have any considerable tendency to prevent it. In opening this convention and with the topic in hand, it seems to me that my words should be general in their bearing. Psychologically, all that pertains to the Christian College and Academy is generic to a Christian education, through and through. Education should· be a projective force. It becomes the educator then to determine the end to be aimed at. If I grind knives keen as razors and throw them out to a crowd of children, the prospective good of my occupation depends on the use the youngsters make of the knives I sharpen. We have a splendid system of education in America, and we have been grinding intellects regardless of the use that is made of them, until they are keen as razors. Moreover we are sending them out into the world with the hint that we are not responsible for the use that shall be made of them, and men may keep a bull-dog or a six-shooter, as they choose, for their protection.

What is the object of public education? Clearly, the making of good citizens. The State does not educate to confer a favor on the father of a family, but to protect itself from the dangers of illiteracy; not because illiteracy is in itself a menace to the Republic, but because ignorance is the parent of vice. The dangers, then, against which our public education is calculated to provide, are the evils of a vicious *proletariat*. How far reaching to this end is our public school system?

I am not inclined to place undue reliance on statistics in ordinary hands, but Mr. Geo. H. Stetson, in a prominent periodical not long ago, made some very significant statements concerning my native State of Massachusetts. No State has carried the public school system to greater perfection, perhaps, but the census of 1850 to 1880 shows a most alarming increase in crime in that cultured State. It very evidently did not result from the influx of the vicious foreign element as we sometimes think. Of the total number of prison population in Massachusetts from 1850 to 1880 two-thirds were native born, and the growth of the crime, surprising, as it may seem, was double the growth of population. The report of the Massachusetts prison commission for one year showed 65,000 arrests for crime. That means one arrest for every twenty-nine inhabitants; and counting five to the family, every six families furnished one criminal. Admitting that a greater portion of the crimes are punished as the years go by, this will hardly leave room for the benefits our system of education is supposed to insure.

As a system of mere intellectual drill this institution is encouragingly strong; as a process in the evolution of upright citizens it is alarmingly weak. As a mere system of intellectual drill I have my doubts as to the right of the State to tax me for the education of the children of my neighbor. If it is just that I teach them, at my expense, grammar and logic, it is apparently just that I teach them the piano and guitar. I think that it is admitted that the justice of the scheme is in the argument that education is the safeguard against vice, and assures us citizens of higher moral endowment. So Herbert Spencer, when he says, "To prepare us for complete living is the function which education has to discharge; and the only rational mode of judging of any educational course is to judge in what degree it discharges such functions." For "complete living" we must have character. Indeed anyone who listens to the demand for universal education will have his ears so filled with "the dangers of illiteracy" that the inference will be inevitable that the ultimate end of all education is, very clearly, character.

If the needs of our Republic demand in our citizen character, the highest education will be that which evolves the highest character. We are slowly approaching the recognition of this fact. Now it is easy, by a simple illustration from psychology, to show that the mere sharpening of the intellect only serves to make an already good man more helpful and a native rascal the keener and shrewder villain.

We live in a time of great scientific activity so far as physics are concerned, but we have been slow to carry the scientific method into educational processes. This may not be without reason. It is only a little more than a hundred years since the human mind was first understood. The greatest philosophers the world has seen lived and died and could never show psychologically why they got up in the morning or went in when it rained. Plato and Aristotle lived and died and never discovered the road traveled by the intellect to reach the will. Aristotle and all the world's philosophers, until a little more than a hundred years ago, divided the human mind into intellect and will—cognizing power and willing power. Under will, they placed the feelings, appetences, and they never understood how the thought arising in the intellect was conveyed to the will and moved the man to action. And yet without that knowledge the intellect is a polar sea, the will an unbridled steed. Others had thought deeply on the theme but Kant was the first to see the gap which the emotions must fill. On one side of the arch he had the intellect—the knowing powers; on the other side he had the will—the volitions, the acting powers; and into the arch between he dropped the key stone, the emotions, the motive power. Ask any tyro in college to-day the fundamental structure of the human mind and he will answer, "Why, of course, the intellect, the emotions and the will." The intellect strikes out the thought, the emotions take it up into the light of experience and move, through desire, the will to act upon it. However brilliant the thought, it is impotent until it has passed through the medium of the emotions and been carried to the will. Yet we educate the intellect and think we are developing human minds. We have developed distortions and intellectual monstrosities too often, instead. One might think forever, but the idea would be barren did not the emotions create pleasure or aversion and carry on the idea to a corresponding issue. If the great object of education be character—men—then it is the utmost folly to train the intellect alone. I think Sir Wm. Hamilton speaks of the emotions as a bridge over which knowledge marches to volition. They are the medium through which knowledge passes. They are, in a figure, a family of Titans and when thought passes into their workshop, it will not go forth until transformed.

They are the real educators. They send forth their pupils with the impress of their own powerful nature. They stamp them with the lofty smile of the sage or the hideous grin of the fool and clothe them with the fantastic garb of the jester or robe them in the purple of a king. "Keep thy heart with all diligence," said the wise man, "for out of it are the issues of life." "Let me make the ballads of a nation, and I care not who make her laws," said an ancient. He knew that however lofty the knowledge wrapped up in reason and wrought into laws, the proper education of the emotions alone would lead to their execution.

Is it not a marvel that knowing the human mind as we do we are so unscientific in its development? We speak of the good hearted man; but we mean a man of warm emotions productive of good motives. All this is a part of the mind. We shall never be scientific in our education until we train the mind with psychological completeness. (Our fathers "builded better than they knew," we know better than we build.) We profess to train and unfold the human mind. But we know that the home of right motives is the emotions and that the emotions are a fundamental part of the mind. We know they are the only elements of the mind that make our knowledge available or useful. We know that they color all our thought and send it out on errands of love and mercy, or missions of hate and vengeance. We know that all education that educates the intellect alone is one sided and so incomplete as to be shameful. We train intellectual animals and profess nothing more. The result is that every immoral man trained at the expense of the state is thereby made doubly dangerous as a foe to the state. What other does Emerson mean when he says "Napoleon was trial of intellect without conscience?" Lacking moral education his Titanic intellect made him a moral monster.

The educational world is just beginning to catch the spirit of the age, and in certain quarters we hear talk about psychological ethics. Let us not disparage the idea, for no one can teach ethics so as to fully develope a human mind and send the man out a pure, loving, patriotic, helpful, charitable citizen of a Republic without teaching a good generous part of the Christian religion, "What does the Lord thy God require of thee but to do justly, to love mercy and to walk humbly with thy God?" That is good religion, and "psychological ethics" will not be able to omit it. You cannot teach ethics without teaching justice and mercy, and Kant, stoic though he was, declared that it would be forever impossible to get a ground work for even law and order without a practical faith in God. You will find Aristotle teaching ethics on the same basis. "Pure religion before God and the father is this, to visit the widow and the fatherless in their affliction and to keep oneself unspotted from the world." Ethics will sit very close to the gospel there; and Jesus himself summed up the whole divine law in the few words, God the first place, the second you and your neighbor. If the German emperor thinks the world is not ready for such ethics let him ride down "Unter den Linden" in the next Demonstration with his motto, "sic volo, sic jubeo," and see what comes of it. I will not say that you cannot teach such "psychological ethics" without teaching first of all love to God; but Janet's works are standard, and he says that you cannot give "any sufficient motive for the performance of duty without a belief in God." Because the unmoral intellect will say: "If it is possible that God is an illusion, why should not virtue be an illusion also?" When some one admitted to President Seely, of Amherst, not long since, that we must soon introduce ethics into our school system, he said: "If you take the best will you not have to introduce the gospel of Jesus?" Daniel Webster could see no valid reason why a few great religious truths could not be taught in our public schools. He affirmed, with reason, that a belief in God, immortality and accountability of man to his Creator, the relation of life in the next world to character in this, could be taught without the least danger of sectarian strife. Since the safety of the Republic depends upon the education of its citizens, the State will not refuse to educate because a few Anarchists would oppose it in the support of the total destruction of government. And if the ultimate end of education is character, virtue and integrity, the evolution of upright citizens, the State should not swerve from its duty, because a few unbelievers are opposed to all religious teachings. The State has sharpened the human intellect until it is as likely to be deadly as a foe as to be potent as an ally. All the scientific skill of the day should be brought to bear upon this problem. When it is, the fact will appear that only a psychological development of the mind will give us the mental poise and balanced character necessary that a government of the people by the people shall not perish from the earth. The growth will be slow. I believe that the next century will see developed the necessity for persistent public training in the fundamental principles of religious life. Then the minds of the young will be more receptive to the more individual instruction in distinctively Christian truths. Meanwhile, that we may insert as widely as possible the true leaven, the Christian world must pour out money for Christian Academies and Colleges where our young can be trained not merely in intellectual gymnastics, but where the intellect, the emotions and the will may have symmetrical enlargement. Wherever there is a felt want, there is either existent or potential, the answer to it throughout all nature. The world has long felt the need of an answer to the great social problems of this century. The Christian Church is our answer. Education psychologically applied, fitting the mind in its fundamental principles for the higher application of positive Christian truth, will alone solve the problem. We are to see this, ere long, more clearly. Then, for the sake of a sentiment, the State will not prefer the ethics of Aristotle to those of Jesus of Nazareth.

THE BUILDING OF A CHRISTIAN COLLEGE.

Rev. Dr. J. K. McLean, Oakland.

For the sake of turning our discussion to its most fruitful issue, allow me to place upon the broad subject assigned me such modifying limits as shall entitle it "The Building of the Congregational Christian College Today in California."

I. The Great Incentive to the Undertaking.

That is to be found in the close relation which exists between such an enterprise and the coming of Christ's Kingdom. Institutions of Christian education have been, from the earliest days, prime factors in Christian conquest and advancement. Christian institutions of learning have stood to the Christian Church both as armory and arena. Prime agencies for providing material of conquest and supplying the discipline requisite to its handling. Thorough Christian men, thoroughly trained in Christian ways, for thoroughly Christian ends—the kingdom of God on earth can never do without them.

1. The Christian college has existed and must exist, as a standing appeal for such men and as a standing preparatory of them. Purely secular institutions of learning, particularly those maintained by the state and held under its control, cannot, in the nature of the case, either incite men to the Christian ministry, qualify them for it, or back them in it. They are disabled from doing so by their very constitution. Experience already shows their tendency to be powerfully in the opposite direction. The Christian institution of education is the reservoir upon the hill-top to which the pulpit is hydrant in the valley. To any effective system for Christian advancement both are essential. The one can be of little avail without the other.

2. The Christian college is demanded not only as auxiliary to Christian faith and a power for Christian progress, but as well for the conservation of true civilization. It is to be, for that purpose, even more necessary in the future, if that were possible, than it has been in the past. This is evident in view:

(a) Of the visible tendency in our age, country, and especially in our State, to materialism, secularism and to the inevitable consequences of these — depraved moral standards and progressive moral degeneracy.

(b) Of the demoralizing tendency of unsanctified scholarship already apparent in these last few years of secularized higher education.

(c) These tendencies have by no means reached their full swing. Left without counteractant from the Christian college and university, they furnish the most serious menace for the future of our country.

II. The Great Inspiration for the Undertaking.

In that striking narrative in the life of our Lord, the interview with the woman of Samaria, it is incidentally recorded, "Now Jacob's well was there." Have you ever pondered that most suggestive circumstance? The well was there, though Jacob who dug it was gone and had been for seventeen hundred years. The man had ceased, his work survived. And not in mere monumental form, as only keeping his memory green; but in vital form, as keeping the earth green. It stood a perennial ministry to daily human life and comfort. Through it, to how many thirsty souls had the dead patriarch ministered cups of cold water. From first to last what a record of beneficence. Jacob himself drank of the well, and Rachel, their children, servants and flocks; then Canaanites, Judeans and strangers; kings of Israel, Saul, David, Solomon; prophets of Israel, Elijah, Elisha, Isaiah; generals with their armies; caravans with their companies. Especially as situated on the great high-way between Northern and

Southern Palestine in the line of the annual pilgrimages forth and back to the Jewish festivals at Jerusalemn, it had been a land-mark, a resting place and welcome fountain of refreshment. Until at last the day came when our blessed Lord himself was fain to rest his weary limbs upon its brink and beg for a draught of its cool waters. To fifty generations of thirst had it ministered relief.

And, brethren, just outside the walls of Samaria, Jacob's well remains today. Through these ages since Jesus drank of it, does it continue its blessed ministry just as for so long before? Every day of every year for almost four thousand years has one man's thought and one man's deed been a blessing to his fellow-man.

What more fitting symbol to represent the wide reaching and long enduring influence of the Christian College! What inspiration in the suggestion! A well of water, not for man's mere physical need and the world's material want, but for man's religious nature and the world's spiritual want—what enterprise more inspiring! What undertaking so sublime!

Such an undertaking is not altogether a vision of the possible, it has been already realized in fact. There are educational institutions, for their time Christian, which have existed almost as long as had the well of Samaria at our Lord's time. The University of Bologna was founded A. D. 425, fifteen hundred years ago. The great schools of Palermo were in existence and famous in 1300. The University of Prague was established in 1348. Vienna, Heidelburg and Leipzig came soon after. Oxford and Cambridge have sent forth twenty-one generations of Christian graduates. Scotland has four universities of four centuries standing; one of these had, not long since, a force of four hundred and twenty-two professors and three thousand four hundred and forty students. What wells!

Then there are Harvard, Yale, Dartmouth, Amherst, Williams, in our own country. Of which institutions President Carter has lately written, "The colleges of New England have been the most potent auxiliaries of the Christian faith." What have these institutions already done, and what more are they not yet to do for the Christian civilization of the world! What incalculable things may not a similar institution accomplish for the nascent civilization of this Pacific Coast!

III. Some Essentials to the Christian College for Tomorrow.

1. *It must be thoroughly a college.* Else it cannot so much as get a clientage. Our problem is to build today—for tomorrow—in California—a Christian College, of the Congregational sort. Now, whatever else it may do without, a college must have a constituency. But the problem of college-furnishing has materially changed since the year 1700, when ten Connecticut pastors brought each a half dozen books and laid them down as the foundation of Yale, and Jacob Hemingway, conning those books, constituted for two years its solitary student. That method of college building, the only one possible then, can no longer be successfully pursued. The conditions have changed, particularly in California. The Christian College built here today and built for tomorrow must be prepared to stand strong competition from other institu-

tions. To be successful, it must have more to offer than the mere fact that it is Christian. Otherwise even our Christian young men will pass it by. For it is coming to be understood, that among the imperative conditions of success in professional life, thoroughness of equipment stands among the very first. Poorly trained men, handicapped today, are going to be handicapped more and more tomorrow. At all events, we shall not be able to persuade our young men to the contrary. Where the educational carcass is, there the educational eaglets are going to be gathered together. That we may regard as settled.

We, as Congregationalists, lack even the questionable advantage in this regard which some other denominations enjoy. We have, for example, lately heard of the man who wants his Baptist College not only equipped with Baptist professors and furnished with Baptist text books, but taught Baptist mathematics and trained in Baptist gymnastics; if he could get them, he would even want Baptist chalk and blackboards and Baptist soap and towels. Unfortunately or fortunately, as the case may be, we are lacking in such denominational spirit. With us even parents can be slightly influenced by denominational considerations in selecting a college, still less our boys.

In laying today in California, plans for the Christian College of tomorrow, we cannot wisely disregard two facts: (1) That the great body of candidates for the higher education in our State are to be prepared in secular institutions. (2) That our great State University and the greater institution now planting at Palo Alto are going to offer educational advantages of the very highest type.

One of the facts suggested to us is that the minds of our preparatory students at large are not going to be particularly prepossessed toward the Christian College as such; the other, that if we are going to enter the educational field with any hope at all, we must be prepared, as regards at least the quality of our equipment, to stand comparison with those other institutions. In quantity we cannot, I think need not, compete; in quality we must or be foredoomed to fail.

Or if upon any ground of conscience, or of denominational preference, a poorly equipped institution could obtain a limited attendance from young men in training for ministers and missionaries and from young women in training to be their wives, it could not do for these young people what needs doing and must be done. The training which is to place the pulpit abreast of the requirements of tomorrow must be thorough and comprehensive. The church is suffering even today for lack of a sufficiency of sufficiently trained men; the requirement for such is steadily, urgently, increasing. The new aspects of social life, already appearing upon the horizon of the future, the new questions, theoretical and practical, which already oppress society but which are to vex it more and more, demand for the pulpit of tomorrow men of widest information, broadest understanding, alertest perception, profoundest sagacity, and most comprehensive sympathy; in a word, men completely equipped every way. They must be men of utmost faculty, full peers with those who are to lead in the other departments of life. And just here comes in the responsibility of the college; as having in training the religious leaders of tomorrow, the Christian

College must be prepared to do most thorough work. There is some truth, and much which is not truth, in the remark attributed to President Garfield, that a pine log with Mark Hopkins at one end and an earnest minded young man at the other is for all practical purposes, college enough. That were possibly true if the younger man were such as Garfield and the older such as Hopkins. But Hopkinses are always rare, and Garfields never too common. Moreover, the conditions which gave to Garfield's utterance its measure of truth are rapidly changing. The vast deal which even President Hopkins could accomplish for the intellectual and moral quickening of young men like Garfield already needs supplementing, and shall need it more and more in the exigent days which are before us.

The Christian College for tomorrow must be thoroughly a college. No half equipped educational apology has a call to be. It would not be for the furtherance but the hinderance of Christ's kingdom. It could furnish only incompetence, where incompetency were worse than naught.

2. *So too our Christian College for tomorrow must be thoroughly Christian. More Christian than that of yesterday.*

(*a*) In order to conserve such Christian life as may be carried to it. No light task today, that task is going to be weightier tomorrow. Out of a Christian home, out of the warm atmosphere of Christian Church, Sabbath School, Christian Endeavor Society, fares forth the immature Christian, boy or girl, into the wider world of college. Not one of us who has passed through the experience, but knows the peril of it. The new atmosphere, more dense in respect to other things than this youth has ever breathed, must be made and kept more dense also as respects this chief thing. The Christian College which is not prepared to be a Christian conservatory, will have no functions tomorrow in California.

(*b*) It must be able, further, to develope that incipient Christian life, in a full length way, along the lines of intellectual and spiritual enlightenment. Not mere good scholarship in a Christian does the world need, but good scholarship which *is* Christian. The two are by no means identical. The various forms of scepticism and unbelief which in these days are settling upon Christian faith, like the white and black scale upon your orange groves, need to be antidoted at their very beginning. The student needs, if ever, a helping hand in the outset of his intellectual conflicts. In language lately uttered by Dr. Parker, of London, "We want human words delivered with divine accent and realities spoken of with human sympathy. I believe in scholarship, I believe in the larger scholarship that goes beyond mere letters and gerund-grinding and all sorts of finessing—the scholarship that knows the thought and spirit as well as the letter; beyond the letter there is an influence or effluence which the mere grammarian can never understand or appropriate." Such scholarship must be bred into experience out of experience, absorbed out of an atmosphere suffused with it.

(*c*) Our college must be equipped also with reference to making in large and loving ways Christian young men and women of those who come there without Christian faith and Christian life. My remarks so far have gone upon the ground that the Christian College is designed chiefly with reference to the Christian ministry. But the church and world tomorrow, are to need as church and world do today, religiously trained men in all departments of life. There is, and is to be, crying need for Christian lawyers, Christian physicians, Christian teachers, Christian farmers and Christian business men. Inasmuch as our Christian College finds its sole reason for existence in this great fact, it will not answer for it to be Christian to only the ordinary measure of the so-called Christian College of yesterday and today. Its equipments must be more thorough than the mere perfunction of morning prayers, Sunday school, bible class, occasional prayer meeting, with some hasty and apologetic glance at biblical literature. It must have in its boards of instruction great-souled Christian men and women, who, by force of personal character and high spiritual attainment can infuse and enthuse those who come to them for intellectual training with spirit like their own. We are educated by our admirations. We become like those we look up to. I know no provision for a college more essential than Christian instructors who are admirable and are endowed with character and aim intellectually and spiritually inspiring.

IV. The Denominational Basis of the Christian College for Tomorrow.

It should be co-operative, not competitive. Interdenominational, not denominational. It is today the standing scandal of Christianity that, in view of the necessity for the existence of the Christian College and in face of the difficulties attending its building and maintenance, all purely denominational considerations cannot be subordinated to the common end. That scandal of today shall appear all the greater in the light of tomorrow. I, for one, can see no good reason why, denominational lines being retained as now, an interdenominational co-operation could not be had which, in every State of our country, should replace a starveling brood of collegettes with one strong, well-equipped, real college, in which the denominational preference of no student need be attacked or wounded.

But if such co-operation be as yet unattainable—and the persistent experience on the part of us Congregationalists, in vainly trying to secure it seems to indicate that it is unattainable—then the next best thing to try for is a college which is Congregational. That is to say, an institution which, while thoroughly Christian in spirit, shall be in its working essentially undenominational. It is to our everlasting credit as institution builders that there exists a noble cordon of colleges, from Bowdoin on the Atlantic to Pomona by the Pacific, in which any student may pass through the whole curriculum without feeling one finger's weight in influence toward changing his denominational predilections. Can as much be said of any other colleges than ours? If not, then ours is the college to build for tomorrow in California today.

THE CHRISTIAN COLLEGE WE ARE UNDERTAKING TO BUILD.

President C. G. Baldwin, Claremont.

Pomona College is, by force of circumstances, a Christian Academy and Christian College combined. It is not intended to cover more than seven years from the beginning of Latin. It does not propose to make university provision, through advanced electives, for those who wish to begin in part their graduate courses at the close of the Sophmore year, but to give a full general course of undergraduate study in Literature, Philosophy and Science. It believes that these seven years of general work constitute a worthy preparation for special studies in professional lines at the universities. We propose to conduct the school in such a way that our pupils shall have every advantage in materials, apparatus, and teaching force necessary to make the most thorough preparation possible for more advanced and technical work. We propose to employ such teachers, and have such regulations, and establish such traditions as shall make these years of study, from fourteen to twenty-one, years of thorough establishment of scholarly habits and Christian character; and shall also hope to aid each student to discover within that period the character and natural limits of his native endowment, and to have clearly presented to him the various forms of useful and needed work, so that if possible his choice of work shall be fitting and worthy. We shall also, and always, present to the students the highest ideal of fitness for lifework and cultivate an ambition to take a full course of special graduate study in the best universities;

and to this end it will be our aim to bring before the students from time to time the highest specialists for the purpose of enlisting the greatest interest, taking care always that these specialists magnify with us the importance of the general preparatory work of the college courses.

This simple program of Pomona College seems to us to meet the demands of our times in a way to harmonize all important interests. It is a plan which utilizes to the full the magnificent endowments of our great universities, not distinctively Christian, by sending to them the best trained material ready to appreciate and use the men and the equipment of the university. It meets in the best possible way the demand for Christian Education, because it takes the immature years for thorough establishment in Christian principles under most favorable conditions. If we have done our duty we can then, if ever, safely trust the graduate of our College to meet the temptations of the more mixed University life, which might easily have wrecked the undergraduate student.

There seems to be no other effective way of meeting both these requirements for university life—good intellectual education and well established character. This is not an ambitious ideal. The college is always in danger of trying to become a university. This must not be. It is folly to attempt such work without large equipment. It defrauds the student because other schools can serve him better in the special technical courses. It is the business of the Christian College to have such an equipment and such men as will enable it to say to any young man: "You cannot do essentially better in these undergraduate courses than you can do with us." This we must insist upon. We cannot rob our children. There is great misconception as to how much is required to conduct such an undergraduate school. This has arisen from the fact that most of our colleges as they have received more means have advanced into special graduate fields of work, and have undertaken thus a vastly wider field than the undergraduate field. A scheme of education is like a circle, you increase the radius but a little and you double the area and the expense.

Confining ourselves strictly to college work we need in chemistry a working laboratory, which I am informed by high authority in graduate work will require as a maximum, less than $10,000 in equipment. We need in Physics enough apparatus to set up a dozen first-class experiments which will require, according to a very high authority in graduate work, but $10,000 in apparatus. For the museum for actual work—not for display—we need place in the hands of the teachers but a few thousands of dollars. The teachers of Literature, History and Political Science must have a few thousands of dollars for books. We are not to have the library of the specialist in all, or even in any lines. The student who does the work before him can wisely confine his attention to the books which are properly collateral to his studies. The specialist and the university courses need the complete library. The professors in college must be teachers, middlemen, men who give up their ambition to become original investigators; men who keep up with the latest but who give themselves unreservedly to their pupils rather than to the private laboratory. This has been done by the greatest teachers of the world. They have written few books, they have made few original discoveries, but they have given themselves to their pupils; have multiplied themselves in a thousand lives, awakened and stimulated by them. We must have a large force of teachers but we can find three noble and true teachers who will give their lives for their pupils for the salary which the rich universities in self-respect must pay for one original investigator. Our pay roll must give us one teacher for every ten pupils; and if we do the best possible work for each pupil we must have more than that. The nearest possible approach to individual attention is highly desirable and here is where money should be used freely. The laboratory method must be used in all lines and this requires many men.

The typical product of such a College is a student trained in mind to do good work with an enthusiasm born of high Christian purpose to serve the world where it needs him most; safe as regards temptations and ready to respond most quickly to the enlarged life of the well equipped special and advanced courses of the University. I do not hesitate to say that such a man will get a greater uplift from the change from the College to the University than the undergraduate ever gets by partial and incomplete electives which precede his proper graduate work. The system is better as an ideal; and within a few years it will be found that a defined line between the College and the University must be drawn. Mongrels will not be tolerated. Their methods tend to pull away the brightest men from a thorough general preparation just as the Business Course will "side track" the brightest men of the Academy. The Business Course has no place in the Academy. The University Course has no place in the College. To define our limits is to aid in our work.

Are our Christian people of California willing to undertake to build such a Christian School as I have outlined? Are they convinced that in education this is the best and the most desirable thing to do? That is the first question, "Is it desirable?" and this convention should help to answer that question. If the answer is yea, and there is no uncertain sound as we voice that word, then I say it is feasible. For what ought to be, can be. God will help us as we go forward with courage and it shall be. If this is a right plan commensurate with our possibilities, surely we must put forth the effort to overcome all obstacles which may oppose it.

WHY A DISTINCTIVELY CHRISTIAN EDUCATION.

Rev. H. A. Staats, Pasadena.

The one supreme test of the proper education of man is the realization of the Divine ideal in him. What is that ideal? A perfect manhood. We may infer this from Nature. Everywhere in the lower material realm, imperfect development points to richest development; immaturity foreshadows maturity. The Scriptures clearly set forth this ideal. I read, "And He (Christ) gave some apostles, and some prophets, and some evangelists, and some pastors, and teachers, for the perfecting of the Saints, for the work of the ministry, for the edifying of the body of Christ; till we all come in the unity of the faith and of the knowledge of the Son of God unto a *perfect man.*" That is, all ordinances, all the variety of instruments employed in the Church by its Great Head have this for their grand end—a perfect man. What is man in his essential nature and present state, and what is perfect manhood, and how may its royal crown be secured? Man is a compound being. Dissimilar elements combine in his structure. Each has its place and rightly developed bears a designed part in his Divine constitution. There is nothing superfluous in man. Every appetite, every passion, every faculty that belongs to his organic nature is useful; yea more, is sacred. He is a physical being and as such is fearfully and wonderfully made. The body is good. Not one function of it is common or to be despised. To assert the contrary is a reflection upon the All-wise Creator. Man is also an intellectual being. His mental powers are so varied and grand that his capacity for progress seems boundless.

He is a social being, with affections which in their kind and degree ally him to the Divine heart; and crowning all he is a religious being, he worships, has a sense of a higher, a Divine, power to which he owes allegiance and before which he reverently bows. This distinguishes him from all forms and kinds of animal life, not simply as higher in degree, but as separate in kind. Such is man as we find him. It is evident that a perfect manhood is the proper, harmonious, development in him of all these elements. Each has its sphere in the life, each may bring a blessing or a curse. Each needs guidance, control. Even the religious faculty cannot be trusted, for though the highest it is liable to the greatest perversions. Take then man with these elements of his being capable of a development the rich blossom of which may be a perfect manhood, and we ask, where is the power or influence which will secure it? We naturally suppose that an all-wise and loving father would make some provision for it. Where is it found? A distinctively Christian education furnishes the answer. It is the great necessity. Christ was the ideal man; and the principles He taught and embodied in His life have in them the essence and promise and power of a perfect manhood. They touch the whole man—body, mind, heart, spirit. They say all you are is sacred; regard each element of your being as such and use, develop, regulate in accordance with Heaven's royal law of love. A Christian education is the only *all-comprehensive* education of the whole man, and therefore has the strongest claim upon our sympathy and support. It dignifies human nature as it leaves no part of manhood unrecognized, unprovided for. It says to every man, however imperfect and degraded, you have a royal birthright, you are a son of God; and while it points him amid his weakness and sinfulness upward to his possible strength and righteousness, it brings near God as the all-helpful, all-loving Friend. Who shall say that the inspiration of such a vision is not needed for the development of perfect manhood? Who will deny that any education which has not this broad scope is *so far defective!* The men whom a Christian education naturally builds up *must* be the noblest men, the strongest men, the freest men, the largest men—in other words, the most perfect men. For they are the men whose every faculty comes under the inspiration and rule of that principle, which is the essence of God Himself, "God is love." The world in its suffering and degradation demands such; for, if character is usefulness, they are the most useful; if character brings happiness, they are the happiest; and from their hearts as from some rich instrument in perfect tune, sweetest notes sound forth to cheer the weary and sorrowing. A Christian character, the fruit of a Christian education, is thus the world's benediction.

THE IMPERATIVE DEMAND FOR CHRISTIAN SCHOOLS.

Rev. E. R. Brainerd, Mentone.

The topic assigned to me is "The Imperative Demand for Christian Schools." However many things may be said on this important topic, there are but five minutes in which to make four points. So I remark: First. There is an imperative demand for Christian schools, because of the secularizing influences of California life. Vast in territory, rich in worldly goods, thorough in school systems and boundless in resources, yet the golden state has but a small minority of Christians. Taken through its whole extent, California is rife in infidelity, reeking in rum, low in morals. Her brilliant future is threatened with inevitable decay. No Sabbath, no sound temperance principles. Greed and Godlessness dominate. The influences on the young are unmistakably harmful. Our otherwise excellent school system is absolutely void of moral or religious teaching. Owing to the make-up of our Educational Boards as the representatives of the people, our teachers are not largely individuals of marked Christian devotion, and those who are, are forbidden, by precedent if not by law, any religious or Christian teaching. No prayer, no Bible; with ideas of God and Christianity studiously avoided, the result can but be bad and only bad. A recent discussion showed that almost no student from our institutions of learning have entered the ministry in the whole history of the State. In California, religious influences are at a minimum; the demand therefore for Christian schools is at a maximum. No one can doubt that we must have Christian schools in California if we would attain a Christian civilization.

But consider secondly, character is grander than education. It is fundamental to the welfare of the individual and the State. Education is the foundation of civilization. Progress and prosperity, science and invention; the refinements of literature and of art; commerce and the assimilation of races into our national life are all due to our splendid system cf public education, and along the lines of practical utility our country has produced citizens of remarkable genius. Liberal education has made our people sharp in wits, shrewd in intellectual prowess and of wide spread mental activity. Though young in history, America is prodigious in the results of her educational facilities, and promises yet mightier attainments for the future. But there is one thing that our constitutional government has failed to comprehend. It is this: That though learning, education, skill and power to apply are a great boon to our citizens, yet grander than intellectual attainments, grander than mortal genius, *is character*. That element of citizenship, that alone, can make us dominant, and without this, genius is but a flash in the darkness, quickly extinguished in the gloom of eternal night. Character alone can establish and maintain manhood and preserve and perpetuate the liberties of the people and the privileges of our free institutions. We are already feeling the strain on this, the weak spot in our body politic. Mere mental greatness and a dazzling civilization must inevitably go down before the destroying power of a neglected and weakened moral life.

To this, witness the overthrow of the world's great nations. Greece and Rome, in the brilliancy of their attainments, literary, artistic and political, far surpassed our own. Their famous schools trained in intellect, but could not control the will. Their orators kindled to enthusiastic patriotism the listening throng, but could never awaken the divine energies of a dead conscience. The eloquence of a Demosthenes was but the death song of a nation's greatness, and in the height of its glory the nation went down powerless to endure. Its citizens had lost the true nobility of the soul. Their experiment of education without character should be our warning. Already on this continent are heard the distant rumblings of threatened dissolution, and without Christian education and Christian character our nation must utterly perish long before we reach their glory and fame. Our only hope is in Christian education. The salt of the gospel alone can preserve our secular life. Paul's ideas and ideals must be our standards of citizenship; the mere knowledge of self and secular forces can never sustain man; the ethics and wisdom of the gospel must conserve. The Greeks reared their glorious temple to Wisdom, and over its wondrous archway was carven in letters of gold, the motto of this philosphy, "Know Thyself!" Her citizens paid tribute at its many shrines; but went forth to glorify lust and exalt their own greatness. But Paul, standing on Mars Hill and lifting his voice above the tumultuous acclaims of the Parthenon unrolled the scroll of the Heavens and over the archway of that vast temple, whose dome is the sky, in letters of living light, he inscribed the supreme command, *"Know Thy God,"*—the profoundest learning, the only standard of enduring power. It is plain that there can be no education without character, and for this reason the imparting of character should be the first aim in any system of education.

Consider now thirdly, Christian schools alone can give us Christian education, and insure in our students a healthy manhood and a strong Christian character. Why? From those we receive our education, we receive our character; the stamp of life is impressed by the hand of the teacher. Countless lives and many famous schools testify to this axiom in educational truth. Hence education and character forming must go hand and hand, they are inseparable. To say that the day school should train the mind and the Sunday school the character is, to say, that we must depend upon the lesser influence to counteract the greater.

To say that the public school should deal with mental growth, and the home develop the soul is to require us to nullify home training by thirty hours a week of contact with the subtle tendencies of secular education and secular educators which, in rare exceptions, must prove disastrous. Education without character forming is suicidal. The discussion about parochial teaching, the Bible in the schools, the separation of church and state, and the founding of Christian institutions of learning may go on till the crack of doom; but you can never divorce character forming from any system of true education. *Character is the imperative demand of the day, in civil, in religious and in political life.* Now, if it be true that character is formed and the bent of life imparted by our educators, then it must follow that the imperative demand of the day is for the foundation and maintenance of distinctively Christian schools.

Now, fourthly, this is just what we have in Pomona College. If you will study the history of our great men, the men who have acheived grand moral victories in statesmanship, in the judiciary, in the pulpit and in the lesser walks of life, you will find that their feet keep step with the tread of that vast army that have come forth from the portals of our Christian Colleges. Follow the march of history through Yale, Amherst, Williams, Middlebury, Dartmouth, Oberlin, nearly all of which, in their geographical situation, could be set down within the limits of our great State and tell me what untold influences have gone forth, and shall perpetually go forth to build for truth and right by a Christian education. These all were founded on the gifts and prayers of those who saw their country's peril and sought the nation's good. Can any one doubt their need and power?

What would our land, our citizens, be today without the conserving influences of these institutions? What these have been in the East we must build on the shores of the Pacific. For ours is to be a colossal civilization; colossal in commerce and civil power; colossal in culture and artistic attainments. A new Greece and a new Athens, a golden age of brilliancy and power. Let us build here a new Antioch and a new Jerusalem, colossal in Godliness and in spiritual grandeur—a golden age of true liberty and celestial power. Let us not be afraid that we shall have too many Christian schools and colleges, but establish and maintain them in the conviction that they are necessary to true education and enduring national life. And let us be especially loyal to Pomona College, the child of our prayers and earnest desires and worthy of our fondest hopes. Let us make her the Yale of the West, sending forth her great men to dominate the land. Aye, let her rival the schools of ancient renown, in learning and spiritual power, surpassing the Alexandrian age and the wisdom of Gamaliel, taking for her standard the breadth of culture, the depth of spiritual discernment and loftiness of moral grandeur revealed in the Perfect Man and putting the stamp of character on countless heroic souls that shall go forth like Paul to make our Palestine a Holy Land.

CHRISTIAN EDUCATION AND CHARACTER BUILDING.

Rev. E. D. Weage, National City.

Every one must be educated. It is not a matter of choice. One might better talk of breathing, digestion or thinking being a matter of choice. There are things we must have whether we will or not. Education is one of them. Education is development of character; character in its mental, moral and physical sides. Everything educates. We have no control over the process. A man may take food or let it alone. Having taken it the result is beyond his power of choice. In that realm God acts, not man. We put the seed in the soil; having put it there we have nothing to do with the result. We may water it. Having watered it we have nothing to do with the effect of the water. God and men are partners. God has His work, we have ours. Every act in life educates. Everything we come in contact with educates; just as every thought changes the structure of the brain so does every experience change character. We cannot avoid it; we cannot alter the fact. Most of our education is unconscious. The young man goes to school to get an education. He gets it. The smallest part of it comes from books. Most of it comes unbidden and unknown through fingers, ears and eyes. A man may listen to good music till he loves it, but he does not realize the process of development. It is not in anything he can see or touch. A man may study pictures till he becomes an artist in soul but he never sees the development in progress. The young man on play-ground, in society, in class-room, forms his character and determines his intellectual success or failure more by what he does not think of than by what he does think of. Physical exercise is good for physical development; but that development is conditioned not so much on the exercise as on the air and sunlight in which the exercise is taken. Exercise in a foul cellar would be of small profit. A man walking in an African forest may take in malaria enough to kill him and not know of the harm till after it is done. The moral and intellectual atmosphere that surrounds college life is far more powerful than all the instruction in text books. We should take special pains to see that these unconscious educational influences are right. We can't hinder the working of such influences. We can put ourselves under right ones. A man who, without the best of reasons, puts himself under the influences of some colleges and expects to come away unharmed tempts God. He might as well swing Indian clubs in a small-pox hospital. Don't jump from the pinnacle of the temple and expect God to catch you. He has better work on hands. A man may study and pray and work for God, and yet treat his nerves so that they shall be allies of the Devil. That is poor policy. It is good policy compared with that which, in his most critical period, when he is striving to build a broad and firm intellectual character, puts a man under influences which, with all their insidious and terrible power, work for ruin. Give us pure air and clear sunlight.

But it is not alone on the moral side of character building that the Christian part of an education is well nigh indispensible. Look at the intellectual part of it. A man, who soaks his body with wine or beer, cauterizes his nerves with tobacco and enervates his muscles with neglect, isn't good for much in a prize fight. What is he good for in the vastly harder contest of brains? Give a man such influences as shall tend to make him care thoroughly and conscientiously for his body as the Temple of God, and you greatly increase his chance of success in brain work. Here is one place where even our Christian colleges are not up to mark. There ought to be no Christian college where special and detailed instruction on the hygiene of brain and nerves is not given. We would have far less poor work and failures and collapses and suicides. Many a man works on after God has written his coming ruin in letters of languor and restlessness and pain that sets all his nerves athrill, and never a Daniel rises to interpret to him the handwriting of the Almighty. Then comes one of what we call mysterious Providences—with nothing mysterious about it, unless it be the indifference of those who ought to have furnished an interpretation to the warning and did not. But, as much behind the times as our Christian colleges are on this point, others are still more so. Not only does the student in a Christian college stand a better chance of building a strong intellectual character, because he is under influences that tend to help him save and use his forces to the best advantage, but because he is likely to get really broader and more thorough instruction. All facts are connected. Things are seen rightly only as they are seen in their relationship. Our fathers saw steam. It did not amount to much. They did not see it in its relation to practical life. They saw lightning. It did not profit them. They did not see it in relation to common affairs. Men see the facts of science and history. These facts are intimately related to the soul and God. What if the teacher is blinded by materialism or agnosticism so that he does not see these relationships? His perception of the character and meaning of the facts is by so much dull. Given a man whose vision is clear, and his view of the facts will be broader, fairer and more inspiring. You see a man working with a microscope. It is a costly instrument. The object he is examining seems dim. He adjusts the instrument; still dim. Rubs the lenses; still dim. He takes the instrument apart and with a few drop. of alcohol thoroughly cleans the lenses. Ah! he sees now. The dirt of materialism and the smoke of agnosticism make bad work in examining the facts of the worlds Give us an institution where they keep the lenses clean.

THE STUDENT MATERIAL FOR COLLEGE BUILDING.

Professor E. C. Norton, Claremont.

You have listened to the President, as he has given for the Trustees and Faculty the main characteristics of the institution, which, in Pomona College, it is proposed to build up; and I think you have all said, "Amen, go ahead, brethren, and when the work proves that it possesses such qualities we will joyfully own it and give it to the world as our tribute to Christian civilization."

But, however high the ideal which Trustees and Faculty set before themselves in this building of a Christian College, however wise their plans and true their hearts, they cannot place it on the level they desire either in respect of mental or of moral life. After they have done their best the tone of intellectual and spiritual activity of the institution will be the average tone of the body of students; and in these days of beginnings, you, pastors, are largely responsible for the students we receive or fail to receive. The real life of the College is in its students; in greatest degree they hold in their power its good name, its prosperity, its influence. The modern college is neither a monarchy nor an aristocracy; it is a democracy, and the students are the *demos* —in reality the governing body.

What one of us did not feel and recognize in our student days that indefinable something that may be called the "spirit of the institution"—an intangible but real thing that had uplifting and restraining power—saying to each successive class, this is the way; walk ye in it. And so the Freshman, without thought of resistance and almost perforce did certain things and did not do certain things because—why, because it's a way we had at old Amherst, or Yale, or Dartmouth, or Oberlin, or wherever else we came under the sway of this ghost of the past. The traditions of institutions long founded are mighty powers, and so far as they make for honorable living and righteousness, mighty powers for good. The Freshman, the Sophmore, the Junior, the Senior, drops into his round of duties, of pleasures, of recreation, yes, even of vices, at what is considered the proper time, because, don't you know, its "the thing" at his college. There can be no change of the internal spirit and life of an institution. It may be developed—it can not be revolutionized. The quality of our student body is then of the utmost importance during these formative days, when there are no traditions of the elders, no way in which things have always been done, no spirit that walks abroad and lays a restraining hand on every brother that walketh disorderly.

The old and very sensible receipt for cooking a rabbit was: "First catch your rabbit." For building up a Christian College the first essential is to capture live Christian students—not simply Christians but students. There is a grave danger for a young college which carries with it the name of Christian, especially just at that time when it begins to gain some little reputation as a good and safe institution, and more especially where all the influence of the great institutions is given to endow us with such a character in the eyes of the people. Here is a very bright student in some brother's church—a boy coming out into earnest Christian life. The pastor perhaps agrees with the parents that it is safe for him to go to some institution carrying a larger name than Christian College. Perhaps neither pastors nor parents always stop to consider that if Christian Education is necessary at all there are duties as well as privileges regarding it, and so, unwittingly, they may help to make Christian Education what not a few would like to see it, a thing of the past.

But here is a boy who "never did hanker very much after being a Christian" and his moral character is getting a little shaky, he has had trouble with his teacher in the High School, and his parents don't quite know what to do with him. The danger is that some friend of the

College suggest that he be sent to Pomona College, where they make so much of religion and the influences are so good. Give us enough such friends and we are undone.

I know we cannot expect to receive the best students if we cannot do the best work, nor, on the other hand, can we be expected to do the best work if we do not have the best students you can send us. The Christian College is not, and must not be made, a home for the feeble-minded, nor a rival of the institution at Whittier. More than any other institution of learning must it refuse to accept those who cannot bring clean papers and refuse to retain those who do not maintain a clean and helpful character, and this is especially to be emphasized during its critical years when traditions are being established and customs formed not easily broken. "This does not have to be a large school," said Dr. Arnold, "but it must be a school of Christian gentlemen." This should be our ideal—not quantity but quality. There is indeed a work we can do and ought to do for the weak, but for the doing of this work we must first have strength and momentum. Green wood is all right if you first have fire enough. But in the present crisis one of your brightest and best is worth to the building up of the college a dozen indifferent students. The first one to go to Pomona College from your community will in general be the type of all succeeding pupils, and will fix for your people their estimate of the character of life and attainment at the college. If this is true, are we not justified in asking for your best—bright students, sound students and such as sleep o' nights.

THE DUTY OF THE CHURCH TO THE INTELLECTUAL LIFE OF HER CHILDREN.

Rev. Lucien H. Frary, Pomona.

Matthew Arnold, a few years ago, in his lecture on Numbers, took the ground that the great defect of our Republic is disobedience, want of respect, and exaggeration, but that there is power in the large remnant amongst our millions to save the nation. The remedy lies in unceasingly multiplying the numbers and efficiency of the remnant. Precisely this, I understand to be the question before us this A. M.

How to increase the remnant of liberally educated Christian minds in America is the problem that inspired the calling of this assembly. We stand in the gate-way of the twentieth century. We do business by telegraph and telephone. We travel by steam and electricity. We tunnel mountains and heave ocean beds with dynamite and rock-rend. We light our streets and warm our dwellings with fires kindled by the force of mountain streams. We have ceased to be surprised by the wonders of mechanical invention, since the civilization in the midst of which we daily act, is itself the wonder of the ages.

At times we are tempted to regard ourselves as only an element of this amazing movement going on before our eyes. Power of every kind is concentrated. Time is wealth. The world does not wait for men leisurely to muse upon its calls to service. Opportunities unaccepted are quickly withdrawn. We listen to men who think straight and see clearly. Definite ideas, strongly held and concisely spoken, are in demand. The untrained mind labors under disadvantages that grow more irksome every hour. Even obscure communities require for their higher needs, the man of broad views and distinctive convictions; while in the great centers of thought and action, the poorly equipped workman finds his burden well nigh crushing. There has always been a pressing need for skilled, solid, Christian men. But never was that need so imperative as at this moment, and in our land. The necessity of popular intelligence and public virtue as a safeguard to the nation has become a commonplace upon all our lips. With democracy made sovereign, and the line between liberty and license delicately narrow; with the growing effrontery of crafty and thieving demagogues; with the multiplied wants and healthy discontent of mankind, brought about by the social and material advances of the past, there comes a loud and urgent call to vastly increase the company of men and women who, by the exercise of mental discipline and moral integrity in the various callings of life, shall help to make America, not only in name, but in very deed, the enlightener of the nations, the pioneer in the vanguard of the hopes of the world. Thoughtless mobs, wreaking their fury upon real or fancied enemies, cannot do this work. Neither is mere goodness equal to the task. The political, social or moral questions of our day will not be solved by selfish schemes or ignorant philanthrophists. The times call for the combination of intellectual and moral power, for faithful men able to teach others, also men of trained mind and educated conscience. No others can do the work that waits our hands. The struggle for material gain grows more intense. In their heat, men cast aside moral scruples as a runner throws off his garments in a race. And yet society can stand only upon the solid rock of rectitude. To tamper with the sanctities of God's law, to consent that anything rather than religious integrity shall rule in human affairs, is to tear off the planks from the bottom of the ship in which we sail with all our goods.

Progress in the conquest over matter bids us learn anew, and continually, the truth that in the world, "there is nothing great but man; in man there is nothing great but mind." A man in one aspect may be a mist, a withering flower. In another he is gigantic, immeasurable, immortal; and he is never so great as when disciplined in all his powers and uplifted by the aspirations of an intelligent Christian faith. "Governments, religion, property, books," said Humboldt, "are nothing but the scaffolding to build a man. Earth holds up to her maker no fruit but the finished man." "Mankind," said Kossuth, "has but one single object—mankind itself; and that object has but one single instrument—mankind again." "Men," said Pericles, "are a city, and not walls." The prayer of every Christian American should continually be, "O God, give us men."

Consider, too, this idea of liberty. What need that millions in this land learn the real meaning of that word. Blessed shall be the men who teach the precious lore that liberty is the office of righteousness, that liberty is self-reverence, self-knowledge and self-control. Blessed, too, shall be the men who, by plain living and high thinking, show the community how simple are the real needs of life and pour silent contempt on the regency of gold. "For departed kings," says one, "there are appointed honors, and the wealthy have their gorgeous obsequies ; but it shall be the nobler lot of these to clothe nations in spontaneous mourning, and to go to the grave among the benedictions of the poor."

Our country needs leaders and commanders of the people. And for these, to the Christian College she must continually resort. But how shall the Christian College honor the draft without perennial supply from the Christian church and the Christian home? In the Christian church and the Christian home is set the center of hope for the saving of the world. The very atmosphere of the Christian College inspires to the broadest manhood. The value of clean, strong lives, is there constantly and everywhere felt, and young men are fortified with every noble purpose. Thus, as Christian ministers, lawyers, physicians, business men; as presidents and instructors in colleges; as scientists, statesmen and authors; as guardians of asylums, reformatories and hospitals; as missionaries at home and abroad, the alumni of our colleges are doing a work so vast, so beneficent that no man can take the measure of it. Educated men who walk with God and invoke his aid in the issues of the hour are clothed upon with a power that shall bring victory to the truth and safety to the Republic. They go forth under the leadership of one who hath on his vesture and on his thigh a name written—King of Kings and Lord of Lords.

In view of these hints I venture to hope that you will assent to the timeliness of my theme: The Duty of the Church to the Intellectual Life of Her Children.

THE PERSONAL FACTOR IN EDUCATION.

Rev. C. T. Weitzel, Santa Barbara.

My subject is the educational force of the personality and companionship of the teacher. The teacher is something more than a live text book on arithmetic, grammar, history. He certainly ought to be. His personality educates as truly as do the facts, laws, or principles he teaches. Is he a mere hireling, doing his work for so much money? He will not give his life blood to his scholars. What lesson will he teach of service? This—it is a matter of money. He must have the dollars. Therefore he must do the service. Service—a hard necessity, nothing higher; that is the lesson he teaches of service. Is he more than a mere hireling—a friend; a lover of his neighbor? His whole manner shows it. What a new conception of service he gives by the way he throws himself into his work. Still, a necessity it may be. But something vastly better, higher, giving a thought, teaching a law, impressing a truth. There is a joy in it. To serve is a privilege. There is something in true service for which money cannot pay. He truly serves who gives himself—that is the lesson he teaches of service. Is the teacher a literalist? Is he bound by the mere letter? Or is he one who habitually catches at the spirit of a fact or principle? The one teaches history as a collection of dead facts and dates. The other as an illustration of eternal living principles, a prophecy of what shall be, as well as a record of what has been. Is our teacher scornful or reverent? His scholars will learn of him the disrespect that lowers the great to our own level, or the humility that exalts us toward the great. Does our teacher hold fast the traditions of the past, or eagerly welcome the new light ever breaking forth? His scholars will learn of him the narrowness which would have us receive spiritual truth through one window only—the Bible; or while recognizing the preeminence of the revelation of the Holy Writ, they will learn to think God's thought after him in the marvelous world of his making, and recognize the voice of God in all human history and in the human reason and the human conscience. Is our teacher's life in thought, aspiration, act bounded by time, or does it reach out into eternal years? He need say nothing about it. To the impressible minds and hearts influenced by him it is soon made known, and they are either left at the low level of those who live by the day to have a good time, and to whom human standards of success and failure are final, or they are taught to ask, not what is pleasant but what is right; not how does this serve my life but how does it serve all life? In a word, the teacher cannot ask a question, explain a problem, administer a reproof, correct an error, without revealing and impressing himself on the scholar.

This factor in education, the personality of the teacher impressed by familiar intercourse with the taught, is not sufficiently recognized in our schools and colleges, though I bear witness that it is to a very large extent recognized in Pomona College. In this respect, on the whole, we have not only made no advance on the methods of the ancients; we have positively lost ground. The Greek philosophers, Socrates, Plato, Aristotle, impressed their personality indelibly on their disciples, by familiar walks and talks with them, singly, as well as in groups. So did the Hebrew Rabbis on their disciples. It is said of Prof. Tholuck, of the University of Halle, that some of the most illustrious German writers of the century were led into the Christian life by him; that in the pulpits and professorial chairs of Germany, there are at present hundreds who are preaching and teaching a gospel they first received from him. Among his papers were found hundreds of letters from students and ministers owning him as their spiritual father. What was the secret of Prof. Tholuck's great success? This: From the beginning of his work as a University Professor, on through the busiest portion of his world renowned public lecturing, he regularly spent four hours a day walking with students, besides having one student at his table for dinner and another for supper. At such times he sought in every way to get at the inner life of his guest or companion. In this familiar intercourse, we are told, "he was full of geniality and overflowed with humor; he tried the students' wits with the oddest questions, and those who enjoyed the privilege of walking with him would retail for weeks afterwards the quips and sallies in which he had indulged. He knew how to draw every man out on the subjects with which he was acquainted. He endeavored to rouse and stimulate the mind from every side, and many owed to him their mental as well as their spiritual awakening."

What, after all, must have been the part of the training of the twelve disciples of Jesus Christ which was most essential, profound, lasting? Shall we not say that just to be with the Divine teacher was the most important factor in their training? Can we not imagine how virtue must have gone forth continually from Him to them in those long walks by the lake and over the mountain pass, during those night vigils, in those familiar talks in the house explaining what was so mysterious in his public teachings? The daily silent influence of that life of perfect piety, sympathy, unselfishness, devotion, heroism, must have worked infinitely in moulding and transforming those fishermen into the leaders of a movement which should fill and conquor the world. We see that the most successful teachers have followed this method of educating by familiar companionship. The best educated nation in the world—the German—follows this method. Let me add a few of the reasons which make this a factor on which we should lay great stress.

We learn largely by unconscious imitation. Some time ago it was a notorious fact in regard to one of our Eastern colleges that its students could easily be recognized by a peculiar gesture which they unconsciously copied from their honored President. A child's walk, his speech, the very expression of his face, reproduces the pattern set by the parent or teacher. He will speak, not the grammar which he has been taught by rule, but the grammar which he hears in the speech of his companions. In recent years there has been a marked tendency toward teaching by objects, illustrations. Abstract truths or facts have been given a body. Pictures fill our current literature so that everything, our magazines and even our daily newspapers, are illustrated. Pictures adorn the bare walls of all the school-houses in our land. Even the stories of Scripture are taught in the pulpits of our land by aid of pictures and the magic lantern. Of much that he teaches the teacher himself is, or should be, the truth in its concrete. He is the live embodiment of it before the scholar, the picture held up before him. We often hear it said that the class companionships of college life are as valuable a training as the instruction of the class-room. If this is so, is there not in the lack of companionship between teacher and scholar the neglect of a force of great possible value?

Another reason for laying stress on the personal factor in education is this: We gain force from contact with a person. A legend tells of a saint of long ago to whom was given power to cure disease, soothe pain, and comfort sorrow without being conscious of doing so. "When the saint went along, his shadow, thrown on the ground on either side or behind him, made arid paths green, caused withered plants to bloom, gave clear water to the dried up brooks, fresh color to the pale children and joy to unhappy mothers."

There is more real truth than we might think in the legend. A bright face, a ringing voice, a firm step—we all know their power to cheer, to rouse. And these are but the outward expression of an inner force, which is ready to communicate itself to us. The enthusiasm of another is infectious. I shall always remember the intense interest in Greek history which was occasioned in our college class by a lecturer who threw himself into the telling of the story.

A sermon is one thing when read in cold blood in your home. It is a very different thing when it comes hot from the lips of a preacher whose soul is on fire with its truths and who summons all his forces of voice, of eye, of personal magnetism to drive the truth home to the conscience. After all, what the world needs most of all is power. Mere knowledge is not power. We want to give force to the thought, the affections, the choice of our youth. It is the teacher's personality more than what he teaches that will inspire. Let the teacher be intellectual, warm-hearted, strong willed, and you cannot give the scholar too much of personal contact with him. Keep the scholar and teacher at arms length—the one on his platform, the other at his school desk—and you sacrifice the greater part of the teacher's power to inspire.

Still another reason for laying stress on the personal contact of the teacher and scholar is one suggested by an admirable paper by President Hyde on "Our Ethical Resources." Speaking of personal influence as one of the resources, he says: "There is a time in the development of every boy when the mind is as sensitive and true to what is best to do and be as the magnetic needle to the pole. Secure his confidence then; find out what form of life's problem he is wrestling with then; show what steps he must take to win the ideal of manhood that is then struggling for recognition; put his feet on the right track then, and he will go right ever afterward and acknowledge his lasting obligation to your friendship and advice."

This time of ripeness and mellowness in a child is often as brief as the same stage in a pear. Approach him too early with moral counsel, and his heart is as hard as a stone. Approach him *after* the period of mellow ripeness is passed, and you find not hardness and indifference any more, but what is worse, the rot of conceit, and the affectation of hypocrisy. The tact and discernment to see just when the child is ripe for a particular line of moral impression is the fine art of moral education and influence.

Now is it not clear that to discern the critical time of peculiar ripeness for an impulse in the ways of wisdom and life the teacher must be *near* to the boy, must know him outside of the recitation room, must be in familiar contact with him? Surely at such a time the personality of a teacher and the degree to which he brings it to bear on a child makes all the difference in the world as to what the after life of that child will be. The highest ideal of the teacher's work is not reached without this personal contact. I think we shall all agree with the assertion that no teacher comprehends his work; no educator rises to the height of his mission who does not perceive, who does not feel, that his first and most sacred duty is to promote good character. Into this undertaking he is to throw his very life. He is to make it impossible for any soul to go out from his charge, without knowing that goodness is truest greatness. Not only to *know* truth, but to *be* true, to be genuine, to be of use in the world—that is, the high ultimate object of all education.

The teacher, who would inspire his scholars, must be able to say in some measure what only He has been able to say in its fulness: "I *am* the truth." If, as Mrs. Browning says, "it takes a soul to move a body," it must surely take a soul to move a soul, and the two souls must *touch*.

THE BIBLE IN THE CURRICULUM OF THE CHRISTIAN COLLEGE.

Rev. F. N. Merriam, Ventura.

In the ten minutes allowed me to emphasize this topic, I shall make two propositions. First, the Christian College demands the Bible; and second, the Bible demands the College.

The first cannot mean that the institutions known as Christian Colleges are calling for the Book to be placed in their course of study, for such is not the case; but, that the Christian College by virtue of its title, ought to demand the Bible as a text book—that its name does demand it. When we speak of institutions like Yale and Williams as "Christian," we mean a great deal. Such Colleges are Christian because founded and conducted under Christian auspices, and because possessing, to a large degree, a religious atmosphere and Christian character. But in the courses of study prescribed by these institutions with much admirable equipment for work in language and literature, history and philosophy, mathematics and the various sciences, there has not been equipment sufficiently admirable for distinctively Christian Education.

The name "Christian" when applied to a college should characterize its class-room. The instruction of a Christian College is bound to differ in some way from that of a purely secular institution. We are met here now to compose a convention of Christian Education. In order to be true to the name of Christ, we are bound to take a Christian point of view in education. If chemists and physicists and mathematicians, we believe that God has weighed the hills and measured the waters; if geologists and astronomers, we believe that God created the heavens and the earth and wrought out the host of stars by number and set them in array; if historians, we believe in the great providence of God and the periods of history designated as "Before Christ" and "In the year of our Lord" are colored throughout by the thought of the great historic figure of Jesus Christ. If we are philosophers, we must be clothed with an intellectual humility because of human limitations and liability to error. In a purely intellectual, as well as moral sense, God's thoughts are higher than our thoughts, as heaven is higher than earth. The earth is God's foot-stool, and all the schools and school men of the world should study at the feet of God. Now if we be Christians in education, it should need no argument to show that we must give prominence to the Bible. When we are reminded of the vital relation between this book and Christianity, we ought to blush for the College man's ignorance of the word of God. Every graduate of a Christian College and man of liberal Christian education, ought to know the general contents of the Bible, and be filled with a profound respect for it. The great Bible idea ought to seem vast in his eyes according to its true proportions. In the name of young men and young women, I appeal for the Bible's place in the curriculum of a Christian College. The church must answer, for the secular institution gives no response. I appeal to Christian schoolmen, not even asking advice of the special scientists, religiously skeptical, however efficient. The unspiritual mathematician, the materialistic chemist, the rationalistic philosopher, however capable, cannot advise us, and however influential must not influence us. They shall not voice our decision. Christians, Christian scholars, must answer and without fear of opposing majorities and shame for minorities, tell us if a College to be thoroughly Christian shall not give high recognition to the Bible in its course of study.

My second proposition is that the Bible demands the College. It is a book so rich and varied in its contents, so large in its scope, so dignified in its nature and so closely allied to the wellfare of men as to demand the scholarly treatment which the College can give it.

Sunday schools, Bible training classes, correspondence and Summer Institutes, all such movements, are excellent, but they express a prevalent need which our College should recognize and endeavor to supply. In the terrific revulsion from Book worship there has been the awful tendency of closing the Book forever, and the church today is wrestling with these two extremes. This wrestling is made on College ground. To give the Bible prominent scholarly treatment in the curriculum, will prove a skillful move on the part of the Christian College in its contest with either foe. On the one hand it would command the intellectual respect of the students for the Bible, and on the other remove the false idea of mere devotion, pietistic charm, and cant that is apt to be associated with the morocco-covered, silk-sewed, sacred Book. It would remove this false idea and at the same time make them reverence and love the Word of God.

This move should be made. The college should give the Bible the time and attention that is due. The time will necessarily be limited because of the claim of the various branches of other work by no means to be neglected. But as much time as possible should be allowed for the purpose of teaching the general contents of the Bible that the students may possess as many Biblical facts as possible. The study would be varied according as Scriptural contents vary, and the time allotted would therefore be distributed through the course. Here portions of the Book should be studied as history; there as literature; here again in the department of linguistics, and there again for Ethics and Religion.

Herbert Spencer ("Education") has ridiculed the false notion of education that is shown in taking up studies without a view to their utility. He never dreamed of being quoted in support of placing the Bible in the curriculum of a Christian College, but his idea does argue for what this paper has to say. There is a practical use to be made of one's knowledge of the Bible and the more complete that knowledge, the greater its utility. A moment ago I suggested that the Book should be studied in five ways in the regular course, side by side with other subjects. The rich literature of the Old and New Testaments will repay careful study. No lover of literature should miss such songs as the Hebrew sang, or such a classic as that sent in a letter to Corinth upon the high theme called by Paul then and Drummond now, "The Greatest Thing in the World."

Considerable is made in College of Linguistics and rightly so. In this department more could be profitably made of the Hebrew and New Testament Greek than at present. Beyond the philological value, there inheres the additional value of their being the chosen tongues that have spoken to the world the oracles of God. Hebrew should be more than "optional," designed for men headed for theological training. It can afford discipline of mind just as well as other languages and in a Christian's view of linguistics, Hebrew is the important language because the speech of Moses and Samuel and Isaiah. Here I might raise the question of a loved and honored teacher, "Why should not college boys read Christian authors, Greek and Latin, as well as pagan ones. Not to the exclusion of the latter, but to a balance between the two?" Is there any good answer? There would result indirect Christian influences from the reading of Christian authors that are not to be disregarded. While assisting the librarian in Hartford Seminary, carrying old volumes from one place to another, I was led to look into one book, because it was so torn and old. The examination was over in a moment, and the little volume was on the shelf again, but in that moment I had caught the opening of a Latin prayer: "O Domine Jesu quamvis indignus." Through all the week that followed and to this day I seem to see that page and to hear a voice from the ages past, praying to my Lord and confessing the same unworthiness that I feel today. The incident does not argue much, but I know that it did me more good than all the "O Jupiters" and addresses to pagan divinities that I have read in classic Latin. It does seem that our Christian Colleges could utilize Christian authors as well as pagan ones.

But think of Bible history. From the Christian point of view, or from any point of view, what phase of the world's history is more important than the grand movement of the Jewish people from Sinai to Calvary? What more suggestive than a familiar knowledge of Jewish history? Here, under the power of Egypt, a thousand years later under the power of Babylon, and at the begining of our era, under the Roman dominion, the Jewish people under the hand of God were ever touching the nations of the orient so that the student of Biblical history has a rich field ever widening for research.

And there are the great subjects of Religion and Ethics. I have not time to more than mention them now; but if our education is to deal with the heart and conduct of men, as well as the head, the Ethics of the Bible should be taught. Biblical Ethics apply to all men. And if the Christian College is to be loyal to truth and consistent to its name, the religion of the Bible should be taught. It is the true religion for all men.

In conclusion this is my thought, that we must always and everywhere be religious and spiritual; spiritual in living, spiritual in thinking, spiritual in teaching. It is this spiritual motive that will give large place to the Bible in the curriculum of the Christian College.

THE REVIVAL OF BIBLE STUDY.

Prof. C. B. Sumner, Claremont.

Why introduce the Bible as a text-book into the day school? Why turn the college into a Sunday school? Not many years ago these questions would instantly have flashed upon our minds, on seeing the subject of Bible study on the program of an educational convention. The movement in this direction in educational centers, however apparent twenty years since, has been gathering momentum, until it begins to be felt to the extremeties of the body politic. Unwonted as has been the quickening of thought in all scientific lines, without a doubt, this quickening has been out of all proportion, in the number of trained minds, and the high order of talent that has been engaged, in the science of textual criticism and interpretation, in the history of the Jews and nations in contact with them, in the study of the Semitic languages, in the interpretation of hieroglyphics, cuneiform inscriptions, and other monuments of the past, in the study of ancient geography, and the exploration of very early cities and temples, all centering in the Bible. The results of these labors have been little short of the marvelous, attracting and fixing the attention of the reading world. So many commanding minds busied with such high and kindred themes, so prolific in revelations, and publishing so abundantly, and in so interesting and fascinating a manner, could not fail to awaken deep interest on the part of students. This interest has become intelligent enough to discover a new meaning in Bible study. It is found that even for the best effect devotionally, the study must be carried on, not in fragmentary portions, primarily for spiritual lessons, but as an intellectual exercise, thoroughly, linguistically, historically, scientifically, with all the side-lights, and last, but not least, as the one wonderful blessed revelation of God.

Under this flood of light from so many directions, and such severe tests of knowledge, we are pushed to the study of the Bible by the almost irresistible momentum of the times. One of the facts disclosed, pressing us to provide for this study in our colleges, is the ignorance of the Bible among educated people. It is a recognized fact, that the average graduate is profoundly ignorant of the Bible, its books, their authors, their setting in history, the light which modern discovery is throwing upon it, its geography, its remarkable literature, its record of human progress, and of a progressive revelation. They have studied it, if at all, only piecemeal, for spiritual profit, and have no conception of its many intellectual lessons, and its inspiration and uplift, when taken by sections and books, and periods, and by its whole, so varied and multiform in its authorship, so divergent in the immediate purposes served, covering so vast a period of time, and yet so single and so mighty in its impression. This anomaly is not easily explained, unless the responsibility rests on our educational institutions, that the Book of books, more widely circulated and read, honored and felt by all classes of society, of more value as a source of history, literature, political, social and moral science, and philosophy, than any other book in the world, as well as the record of God's revelation, and his salvation, is less intelligently and thoroughly understood by educated men and women than the prominent literary works in either the living or the dead languages. Professor Burroughs, of Amherst, does not hesitate to say, speaking of the graduate who has been thus educated in other literature but not in the Bible, "Indeed it is often quite true that his Bible would be worth more to him if he were not educated." This recalls Luther's declaration, "I fear that the universities will prove a great gateway to hell unless the professors therein labor faithfully in the word of God." President Wm. R. Harper, than whom no man knows more of student life, says, "The ignorance of the Bible among intelligent young men would be amusing were it not most shameful."

The study of the Bible presses upon us also, because the average student, ignorant of it as he is, *must* study it, if at all, in college. Amazing as it seems, this is an accepted truth, even with Christian students, by those who have given the matter their attention. When, think you, will he study it? How often does one, in the rush and worry of professional or business life, with all the claims of church, society, general literature and politics, take up any intellectual study to which he has before given no study? It goes for the saying, that to this same average student, Christian though he be, the Bible is to be, as Professor Burroughs has put it, "throughout his future a sealed book intellectually, and very largely a sealed book devotionally." Can a college afford to send men and women out into the world with such a future? The study of the Bible is further pressed upon us because it is not only fitting that the Bible be used as a text-book, but it is unreasonable and anomalous that it is not so used. "The study of the Bible," writes Ex-President Seeley, "is the most interesting of all studies, and the most important. Whatever we may think of its origin, or its contents, no other book has had such wide relations to the history of mankind, and, judging from its effects alone, no other book has such power to stimulate thought, and to discipline thought." We wisely study Heroditus, the father of history, and Tacitus and Livy; have we not as much reason to study the books of the Bible, the fountain heads of history? Where, too, is the philosophy of history so admirably drawn out as in the Old Testament prophets, the gospels and epistles of the New Testament? Every good lawyer studies English common law and old Roman law; will he pass by God's law as handed down through Moses, whence the most valuable principles of English common law and Roman law were derived? Daniel Webster said, "I have read the Bible through many times. It is the book of all others for lawyers." Every scholar becomes familiar with Cæsar's Commentaries. Is there nothing of interest and inspiration in Joshua? Shall we read Homer, Virgil, Milton, and not read Job, David, Isaiah?" "There are no songs," said Milton, "comparable to the songs of Zion, no orations equal to those of the prophets." "Simply for its literature," wrote Henry M. Field, "apart from its moral teachings it (the Bible) is immeasurably superior to any other book antiquity has left us." "As a classic," wrote another able editor, "the Bible is wholly unapproachable by another." * * * "I hold it to be impossible for a writer or speaker to attain his best, or even any considerable eminence without it." We insist on our students pondering over the history of modern and ancient nations in the interest of political science. Is there nothing to be learned from the Hebrew theocracy? Dr. Abbott says, "It seems to me an absurd anomaly that a man should come out of college, supposed to have a liberal education, and know about Greek and Latin history, whose relations to American life and institutions is measurably remote, and know nothing about Hebrew history, whose relation to American life and thought is very direct." Will any one question whence

Savonarola, Luther, Calvin, William Prince of Orange, John Knox, John Robinson, Abraham Lincoln, drew their wisdom, their inspiration!

Sociological questions command increasing attention. Are we not forced to the Bible for the data on which to study this science for the first four thousand years of the world's progress? But apart from the sources of information, where can we find such perfect idyls, such expressive bits of family life, such revelations of the individual soul, by which we may study the springs of human society, with reference to prosperity and adversity, happiness and misery, as well as the great principles of right and wrong? Is not President Carter correct? "The people from whose moral and religious reservoir all the world has drawn the tonic of daily social life, is worthy in its origin and history, in its ritual and its literature, of study in the college course."

It is essential that the student should be acquainted with the teachings of Plato, Aristole, Cicero, Sir Wm. Hamilton, John Stuart Mill. Is there not philosophy equally profound in Solomon, Isaiah, Micah, John, Paul, and most of all in Jesus, the Christ? "We count the Scriptures of God," declared Newton, "to be the most sublime philosophy." On listening to the reading of the fourth chapter of the first Epistle of John, Ex-President Mark Hopkins exclaimed, "There is more in that chapter than in all the philosophy of the ancient world."

The grand distinguishing character of the Bible, as the record of God's revelation, redemption from sin, and restoration to the favor and fellowship of himself, urging us to Bible study, is yet untouched. Will an unprejudiced man hesitate to give a large place to its claim in this respect? Surely in this land where one-third of the voters are church members, and enough of the others, according to Joseph Cook, sympathize with them to insure their vote on great moral questions, the Bible does not count for less than Confucius to the Chinese, the Zendavesta to the Parsee, the Vedas to the Hindoo, and the Koran to the Mohammedan.

These and like reasons have pressed so strongly that at length we recognize a widespread demand, which is fast becoming irresistible, to make the Bible a text-book with its allotment of time and hard work in our colleges. What means this body of students, numbering into the thousands drawn from nearly every college in our land, with many more from the oldest institutions in other lands, voluntarily associated for Bible study? The character, as well as the number of these students gives strength to the movement. Through its influence, the request has come from the students themselves that thorough study of the Bible be provided for in the curriculum. The Amherst Literary Magazine says, editorily, "We believe we voice the sentiment of the student body in directing attention to this need. We claim that every well educated man should be acquainted with the facts and proofs of Christianity." Truly the students and our leading educators are at one. Hear President Bartlett, "It is a book too centrally and vitally related to history, literature and civilization to be omitted from a course of liberal education." And President Knox, "Surely in this day, when as never before, the public mind is concerned with the history and contents of the Bible, no one can be considered educated who has not a somewhat full knowledge of the subjects directly and indirectly suggested by the sacred volume." Some of our foremost Eastern colleges have yielded to the demand and provided for this study in their curriculum, and in their libraries. Pomona College has felt the demand and has begun systematic work in the line of Bible study with all its pupils and is already placing valuable books of reference in this department upon its library shelves. Far more work must be done in the near future, if we make Pomona College a worthy tribute to Christian civilization upon the Pacific Coast.

THE NECESSITY OF PROMOTING CHRISTIAN EDUCATION BY PRIVATE BENEVOLENCE—NOT A DISADVANTAGE.

Rev. A. E. Tracy, Ontario.

It is conceded by all that the State cannot give us a Christian education. Why it cannot, we need not now consider. We are met with the fact. If then we are to have Christian education, it must be by means of schools established and sustained by private benevolence. The subject, as worded on our program, indicates that there are disadvantages, or at least seeming disadvantages, in this fact. I am to attempt to show that this seeming is not real. I have time to name and reply to only four of these apparent disadvantages.

1st. "There are so many and so loud demands for the money of Christian people that it is a pity to have so much of it turned into these educational channels. If the millions of dollars expended in Christian education could be put into evangelistic and missionary work, the Kingdom of God could be hastened more rapidly." It would at first seem a real gain if the State would give us what now is had by the generosity of individuals, thus releasing great sums of money for gospel work. But there is a compensation. Gifts to our colleges, especially small gifts, mean sympathy, prayer, interest in their success. An atmosphere of Christian devotion, sacrifice and service, is created in which the noblest, truest manhood is likely to develop. The difference in the influence of a school cared for by a legislature, or even a single great donor, and one held in loving remembrance by a multitude of true, praying ones can scarcely be less than that on a child cared for by a hired nurse, and one to whom a devoted, wise mother gives the fullness of her love, wisdom and prayers. Note the atmosphere of Amherst, Williams, Beloit and Grinnell, and superlatively Oberlin. It can largely be accounted for by the lives built into these colleges, lives of donors, as well as teachers.

2nd. "As a rule, colleges dependent on private benevolence, lack complete equipment, cannot have the fine buildings, apparatus, and all things needful to the best work and broadest culture." We are in danger of setting too high an estimate on externals as essential to a full education. The tendency is to try to draw students by the appliances helpful in education, rather than by the personality and educating power of the teachers. I think an unbiased investigation would show that Christian Colleges have had a larger proportion of teachers who were fitted to mold characters, who counted it a large part of their work to do this, than State Institutions. These Colleges have been really better equipped for work than some great institutions with large sums of money to expend for apparatus. There is a reason for this superiority in the personnel of the faculty in a Christian college. They have accepted positions in them because of the opportunity for doing an important work; the pay, the chance for original work, has not attracted them, but the possibilities of usefulness. Such characters mold others to a like spirit of devotion to high ends.

3rd. "To depend on charity fosters a pauper spirit. The student is continually reminded that he is receiving something for which he does not pay; his education is made possible by the gift of those upon whom he has no claim."

A sufficient reply to this objection is an appeal to facts. Where can you find men of more manly, independent spirit, than among the graduates of Christian Colleges? The spirit of self-help and reliance on their own powers is marked. Because they have received something so precious that many have gladly sacrificed to give it them, they feel the obligation to make their education of greatest use to the world. Personal honor is appealed to more strongly than where the State has educated.

4th. "A college dependent on private benevolence must keep its president or financial agent in the field, and so the college is viewed in the light of a beggar."

This may be a disadvantage to the man, but not to

the public. We must get above the thought that it is a necessity to be regretted that the needs of the world must be kept continually before the people. A good college agent or president is an educational force. He gives the people a better understanding of the possibilities open to the church through her educated youth. I do not believe there is a church in Southern California where the President of our College has spoken, that has not been benefitted by it. The minds of the people are drawn toward the college, and they begin to talk of the possibility of sending their sons and daughters. Thus the influence and good of the college endures. As well count it a disadvantage that our Missionary Societies keep representatives from the field among the churches to inform and inspire them as to the work doing, and to be done. The more closely the homes, the churches and the college are linked together the better. The college must be taken into our closets, remembered at our family altars, in the public worship. The churches are to be its feeders, both with students and money; in return it will lift the standard of true manhood before the youth in our congregations, and become an inspiration to the intellectual and spiritual life of all our communities.

PECULIAR CONDITIONS IN SOUTHERN CALIFORNIA WHICH MAKE SPECIAL DEMANDS UPON POMONA COLLEGE.

Rev. T. C. Hunt, Riverside.

The time was when, if a man desired to come to California, the thing to do was to get a good team of oxen or mules, a strong wagon, load it with provisions and join a caravan, creeping over plains and mountain fastnesses till the welcome breakers of the proud Pacific should greet his weary eyes.

You and I did not come in that way; and considering the time when we did come, and our purpose in coming, we should not have been counted wise if we had. If I know the difference between success and failure in individual life, or in that of any corporate body, it depends on hardly more than two principles; adaptation and application. Adaptation comes first; for, figuratively speaking, men often show a deal of energy in butting their heads against a wall, but their effort is never attended with any worthy success. We are striving to build a college, what are the peculiar conditions to which we must adapt ourselves, if we would have our effort issue in worthy success?

1st. We live in a region where population is to be grouped in dense settlements; holdings for those engaged in agriculture are to be small; all the people are to enjoy most of the privileges usually enjoyed only by those in cities or large towns in the East. Our system of water supply and kinds of produce we raise, render this statement self-evident.

2d. We live in an age when no father can render a just account for his charge, who does not provide for each of his children, at least so much education as may be gotten in a good high school. Great misfortune or extreme sickness alone can excuse a father for allowing a child to enter any calling of life without so much of opportunity; he cannot render his account as a good citizen of this Republic, nor can he command the respect of his children, in this day and age of the world, if he does not provide them with so much of opportunity. If children are reared with this thought held constantly before them, that till they have so much of study they can hardly tell what they are good for; if this expectation on the part of the parent is impressed from early life; it will be hardly more difficult to keep the great body of children at school so long, than to keep them there till they have learned the rule of "Three."

It follows then that every settlement in Southern California must have its good high school; it follows then that every good and worthy citizen will support that school and do all he can to make it what it should be. What education we count necessary for all, we must do all we can to place within the easy reach of all.

To my mind there are four distinct reasons why our college must, in no sense, conflict with, or even compete with the high school system in this part of the country.

1st. If we take our children from these high schools and place them where we imagine they will do better and are safer, we do about all it is in our power to do to weaken the schools and discourage those who have not too much encouragement at home. Let a class graduating from the grammar school find many of its members going off, and those who cannot go will be sorely tempted to drop out. Let the class try to go on bodily, and parents and pupils will make great sacrifices to keep the class together, and make it the best the school has ever sent out. Many, having completed the high school course, will then have found the educational instinct and ambition, and cannot be prevented from going farther. Every man who has ever taught will feel that the weight of this argument in favor of supporting the high school cannot be exaggerated.

2d. If we take our children from these schools we lose all the influence we might have to mould the schools. There is no more forceful argument with a teacher or with a school board than " my child is here, and nothing but the most refined morals and most profound respect for religion can be tolerated." But take your child out, and your influence is largely gone, and rightly so. This loss the ministers and laymen of our churches cannot afford, unless some great and manifest advantage can be found, to more than counterbalance. Here is most certainly an obligation to *Christian civilization*, which it will require the largest *personal advantage* to overbalance.

3rd. If a college is to fill the place it ought to fill, the teachers of our public schools must be its friends. They have it in their power to do us immense good or harm. I had almost said that they have our success or defeat in their hands, and in a sense, even this is true. We cannot expect them to be our friends if our influence is to weaken and deplete their schools. It is not to be supposed that any one will work in a school that he does not believe in; not anyone who regards his life of worth. Such an one will not favor an institution whose influence is to harm a system of schools, trying to reach the great body of the children of our Commonwealth with some measure of higher education.

4th. If the High School can do this work, we will not say as well, but with a fair degree of efficiency, and reach a far larger number than could be reached by academies, or fitting schools, our plain duty is to the High School; if for no other reason to save benevolent money, for distinctive Christian work which the State can never do. We, who are a part of the State, supporting it and deeply interested in it, should not only allow the State to do all it can, but should encourge the State in every way to do this.

You have seen the words of Prof. Northrop to this effect. He was asked how we are to keep up the supply of an efficient and educated ministry, and in substance he replied: We must not run in and do the work that the State can do equally well, but reserve our means and energies for that work which is our peculiar charge. I firmly believe that it is high time that this word was passed along through the length and breadth of our land. Because academies were once the thing when communities were poorer, and the population more scattered. it does not follow that they are now the thing. But I must pause, I am speaking particularly of Southern California. A few objections to the position I have taken are worthy of note.

1st. "The moral tone of these schools is likely to be so low that we cannot afford to risk our children." Suppose the moral tone is not the best, the high school has come to stay; shall we give it over to those who care little for morals, and such as are obliged to patronize them, if any higher school? A little study would show that this would be a very short sighted policy, and finally put the Protestant church about where the Roman church now stands, in relation to High schools, at least. I need not pause to show how short sighted this policy would be, endangering the morals of the community at large, and finally reacting on us. We are in the world, it is wise to stay with it with all our forces, doing what we may to mould it. But is the danger so great after all? Our children still under our roofs and in the shadows of our churches? Who has not met the body of our public school teachers, and felt that a nobler body of men and women could not be found in any calling or profession. Bad ones there are, no doubt bad, but who has never heard of a bad minister, who, in someway held his ground. How careful these teachers commonly are—how little chance for evil communication, if parents are equally careful. The greatest danger comes before the children reach the High school rather than after. Most of us are hardly willing to allow our children away from home till they are old enough to be through the High school. We deserve so much of their lives, and when they go away to school, the rule is that the home life is at an end.

2nd. The standard of scholarship is too low, we can not build the college we would, and have it begin where the High school ends. That may be. I would have a fitting school at the college as a supplement to these High schools, at least for the present. But I would so arrange the course of study that it would fit on to the best High schools. Some may say, such would not be the best college course; but we are not working for that, as a first requisite. Solon, after ten years of search for laws for the Commonwealth he loved, is said to have returned to present them for adoption. When asked in surprise, if these were the best laws he could produce, he replied: "No, but these are the best laws the people can receive." So I take it that we are not building the best college that can be built, but that one which at this stage, will be of greatest service to the civilization which it is supposed to serve. Thus, and thus only, can we prepare for the college we would build, if the people are not now prepared for it. I would make the curriculum of both the preparatory department and of the college, with an eye to the best High schools of our part of the State.

Perhaps you know that the building of a Christian college in Southern California is no less a grave undertaking than it has been in the past. Two universities we have, with practically unlimited resources, men from each of them, several times a year looking over our High schools. They are able to present inducements to students to go with them, and they are not slow to do it. They are men too, of practical standing and ability; they understand perfectly the importance of making the step easy from the High school to the University. They are anxious to raise the standard, but careful not to sever the connection. The teachers of our public schools are their friends, and understand the advantages they present. Who of our pastors in Southern California has not seen students go to those Universities this last year who, they felt, would have been better off at Pomona College. We may educate the children of a few of our ministers and the most pious of our deacons, we may educate them away from the world, so that when they begin life they will find it impossible to make the connection, and benefit themselves or the world, but if we compete with these other schools and make toward the mark we have set for ourselves, just now we must understand it, and act up to our knowledge. We must have the wisdom of the serpent, with the harmlessness of the dove. Without adaptation there is but one end, with it there is but one: They are the antipodes of each other: Failure! Success!

EDUCATION—PRACTICAL AND CHRISTIAN.

Rev. Thomas Hendry, Park Church, Los Angeles.

"What we are fixes the limit of what we do." Grant this and how important is education! To do something in this world of needs and possibilities is the aim of every true man or woman; yet what we do is limited by what we are, and this again by heredity and education.

The plea that is made for education is that it extends the limit of possibility. As the fishing limit from our shores is three miles, and beyond that, as a nation, we have no jurisdiction and all may catch in deep waters, so there is a natural limit to our powers as strong as this national law; but education comes to the youth as the craft which shall carry him or her beyond the three-mile limit and open the treasures of a great deep.

"No life is unmusical," it is said. "It is supplied

with strings and reeds, but there is no hand to touch the vibrating strings, there is no breath to move upon the reeds."

How many lives unmusical, unresponsive, have been stirred from the lethargy, which is the common heritage of all by the voice of the "Alma Mater!" How we look back on the halls where we first broke the silence of our own lives and awakened to the fact that there were strings in our nature, capable of wonderful harmony, which had never been touched as yet—that there were reeds in the God-given organ that as yet had never known of this breath from above! You remember the story of Mozart's first experience with the organ, in the monastery of a little town on the Danube, at six years of age; how he left his home in Salzburg and with his father started on a course of travel. All day long they had been sailing down the majestic river, past crumbling ruins, frowning castles, cloisters hidden away among the crags, towering cliffs, quiet villages beyond the trees. The little company of monks were at supper in the refectory of the cloister, the father and Wolfgang went into the little chapel to see the organ. The boy gazed with awe upon the great instrument looming up in the shadows of the empty church, his face lit up with satisfaction; with wondering reverence he moved about it. "Father, explain to me the pedals at the organ's feet," said the lad, and the father did so. Then pushing aside the stool he stood upon the pedals and awoke the solemn gloom behind him. He heard nothing, he saw nothing, his face lighted up with impassioned joy. Louder and fuller rose the harmonies streaming forth till at last they seemed to reach the sunny shore on which they broke, then a riple of faintest melody lingered in the air and all was still. What the organ was to young Mozart the College and University has been to many a youth. But alas! the idol is found to be of clay, "the once fine gold has become dim." Education will not save. An intellectual people may be an unrighteous people. Greece was first in arts and letters. College and University may but fit a man to be a greater villain, to be a more eloquent seducer, may increase his power to destroy. We need more than education; we need Christian education; we need such a college as Pomona College that the youth of our churches may be under wholesome Christian influence while they are laying the foundations for a business training; we need a full stream of youthful life, vigorous in Christian thought and action, believing in God, strong in their loyalty to Jesus Christ and the Bible, to flow out into the Godless life of California. We need young men in our colleges who can impress their fellows with the idea that active Christianity, ardent love for Christ and the souls of men, is not incompatible with high scholarship; we must save our youth from the leprous touch of infidelity and skepticism by contact with those glowing with a Christian experience, their own, yet able to compete with those whom they would influence. Such men must come from our Christian Colleges.

The Young Men's Christian Association recognizes this when they have in their gymnasium class a few earnest, Godly, thorough going young men, who jump high, and box well, to give the young men who have an idea that Christianity is rather effeminate and connected with dim cathedral light a new idea, viz: that Christianity is now thing of every day life, that he must be alert, or this Christian young man, who will not swear and prays in meetings, will out-jump him; that this man who will not visit the billiard halls or dance houses because of his religious convictions will, unless he is on "his taps," give him a sound trouncing with the boxing gloves. He learns to respect those who can beat him at his games, and with respect for the man goes unconsciously a respect for the Christianity which has made the man.

But there is one other rock on which we may founder. There is danger that our education shall withdraw us from "touch" with our fellow-men. Nicodemus said of Christ, "Thou art a teacher come from God." He taught men, especially twelve men; and how thoroughly they were equipped for their life work! Yet he was no "recluse," a man among men was he. "John came neither eating nor drinking," "but Jesus was one who sat at meat with them," "a friend of the publicans and sinners."

The education which leaves us high and dry on the bank is a failure; we must be in the stream with men, we need our "horse sense" after we have gotten through the College and University, and the education which takes this from any is a "mis-nomer."

Our prayer is that this educational institution in whose interests we are met today may be an educational institution of high order, fitting young men and women for university life, business life, mechanical life, yet withal a Christian institution in the truest sense and a practical school.

THE CURSE OF AN EDUCATION WHICH IS NOT PRACTICAL.

Rev. J. H. Collins, Third Church, Los Angeles.

I would be the last one to attempt to discourage a boy or girl from acquiring an education. Indeed I would be sorry if any one word or act of mine here today, or elsewhere at any time, should leave the impression that I would place a low value upon education. I regard an education as capital on hand or stock in trade, and if not properly used becomes a curse.

An education that tends to take a man away from the world and the work of helping humanity, is certainly a curse, and should be discouraged. There is no doubt in my mind that it would have been a blessing to the world had all the principals in both sides in the now famous Andover controversy been left uneducated. I have often thought what a pity that their opportunities for acquiring an education had not been given to persons of more practical common sense; and I say this, though one of the foremost men in the affair has proven a very dear friend to me. But when an education comes to the nicety of neglecting the world and its need of work to indulge in hair splitting controversies of non-essentials, it may safely be labeled a *curse*.

Next—I think an education which is all one-sided, however thorough, is a *curse*. I take it for granted that the great use of an education is to enable us to teach. We may not do so in the pulpit or schoolroom, for there are various other channels through which we may teach.

Now suppose that we become very familiar with the thing we wish to teach, and in doing so we have alienated ourselves from the people whom we wish to teach, we do not know their ways, and we are not familiar with the mould of their minds, we can teach them but little, if any, although we may know a great deal which we would like to teach.

That men and women have been rendered useless, yea, worse than useless, by the overdosing and cramming of purely book-knowledge is a fact, and a lamentable fact, to which there is altogether too much evidence all about us. We may be in touch with great men through study of their works, but the current of knowledge gained thereby cannot be transmitted to humanity, unless we are also in touch with humanity, and the best education possible will not make a man useful if he is not thus in touch.

I am glad that I know enough of the workings of Pomona College to be able to assure you that it does not propose to educate young men and women after such a fashion. From personal acquaintance and contact with its teachers I am sure they are helping boys and girls to acquire a practical education. It has been my privilege to send to the College a young man and a young woman, and no one but teachers fully in touch with poor, needy humanity, could do for a boy or girl what the teachers of Pomona College have done for them, and had I the money to give, I would send a score or more of my young people there to be educated after a fashion, which would not prove a curse, but a blessing to the world and its work.

OUR STEWARDSHIP OF THE MIND.

Rev. O. D. Crawford, Monrovia.

A certain man in Connecticut dreamed a dream in which he passed through a trial for murder. Many witnesses were examined, and eloquent pleas, hours long, were delivered. At the end of three weeks, he was convicted and sentenced. While on the scaffold, protesting his innocence to the last, the trap was sprung. The rope broke, and he ran away. He was pursued by the people and the police, but eluded them until nightfall. Then he ventured to his home; found a gang of ruffians in possession; killed one of them and drove the rest away. Then he awoke and found that he had passed through these protracted sufferings, and the three weeks' trial while sleeping three minutes.

This dream affords us a glance at the superiority of the mind to time, space and matter. By so much is the mind entitled to leadership in all activities, and precedence among all objects of culture. The intellectual faculty pioneers our movements. The moral judgments keep even wing with the flight of thought.

The immediate objects in view in the process of symmetrical training are the increase of the power of clear thinking; the accumulation of stores of knowledge; and the utmost facility in the use of our powers and possessions. The ultimate aim is either self-glorification, or the pleasure of the King.

Stewardship of the mind recognizes the ownership and prerogatives of the Creator. Emerson says that no one but Jesus Christ has ever appreciated the value of a man. That value consists in moral and intellectual worthiness. Mind-work on the field of matter has at last secured, in the present century, a recognized place among the industrial and producing forces. It enhances the value of manual toil, and creates a market for its products in the refinements of civilized society. Its work on the field of ideas ranges the depths and heights of science, art and poetry; of music and sentiment, in which man finds the choicest experiences of life, the glory of his being. The voices of nature and Scripture credit these powers to the Supreme Intelligence. To give up the false claim to the ownership of one's mind, is to yield one's self to the ruling purpose of a sustained act of perfect loyalty to God, which says "whose I am and whom I serve."

Stewardship disclaims the right of even a renter. One who rents a piece of land or a house, can use it for himself, but a steward is managing the business for another. A renter keeps to himself a share of his earnings, but the steward turns over all gains to his employer. The ideal education trains every faculty as the property of God and adds all the increase to the original stock.

The faithful steward is governed by the wishes of his employer. He asks for instructions and receives them cheerfully; he enters upon no plans of his own without approval; he executes orders exactly; he transmits help to others who are dependent upon his master. Here stands Pomona College in the midst of the churches, asking for instructions. Her title to our support lies in her spirit and practice of inciting our youth to enquire after God's wishes, and to will His will; in her efforts to make the mind the master of the body and of nature, according to the law of the Kingdom.

Stewardship lays emphasis on responsibility. The superior man freely moves toward the post of Judgment Day with every mental sail filled with the steady gale of love. The average man needs to feel the pull of duty's cord whose other end is the windlass of the Judgment ordeal. If we can get the mind of the youth saturated with the conviction that they are to give account to God for their use of themselves, we shall have reason to expect a smaller generation of ne'er-do-wells and bummers; that fewer business men will be boomers and stock gamblers, and that more professional men will be incarnations of conscience.

Therefore stewardship also signifies carefulness. Painstaking, so annoying to the flesh, and fatal to the love of ease, is the track of progress. The careful steward looks to each interest and overlooks none. In State Schools the moral law may be impressed by prudential motives; but its claims are never adequately presented, and never met, except where its roots are shown to be imbedded in the will of God, and watered from the fountain of his open word, and fruited in the life and words of the ineffable Christ.

The faithful steward also studies for the honor of his master. Not content with carrying himself as a servitor, he sounds the praises of his Lord. He has escaped the snares of the flesh and ambition with a joyous heart and a clear mind. A ready witness in an Irish court was "unwilling" on the cross-examination. His excuse was that the counsellor's questions put him in a doldrum. The

Judge repeated the word "a doldrum. What is that?" "I can tell your lordship," said the witty counsellor, "a doldrum is a confusion of the head arising from a corruption of the heart." The doldrum disappears as fast as men give up all their faculties, as trusts, and to the service of God, saying with the poet Bailey: "We live in deeds, not years; in thoughts, not breaths; in feelings, not in figures on a dial. We should count time by heart throbs." Thus can we love God with all the mind.

COLLEGE EXTENSION.

Prof. Frederick William Phelps, Eagle Rock.

Whether it be viewed from the standpoint of the College and University, or from that of the general public, the modern improvement, commonly known as University or College extension, is equally to be admired. The only wonder is that it did not long ago become a power. It is impossible at this time to sketch historically the growth of the extension movement. I can only attempt to describe its leading features and to show its adaptability to our College and people, *here* in Southern California and *now* in this year of grace 1892.

The Church believes in education, mental training, stimulation to lofty thinking, cultivation of a passion for knowing the truth about things as an essential weapon in the armament of aggressive Christianity; and the tokens of this faith are found in our Christian Colleges and Academies. We urge the higher education not only upon those preparing for the ministry but upon all alike. In the case of the vast majority, circumstances render College residence a thing impracticable. What is to be done? Shall the College be content with reaching the few? Or is it impossible in some way to utilize the resources and equipment of the College for the immediate benefit of a much larger constituency? Experience answers. If the mountain cannot come to Mahomet, it is both advisable and feasible for Mahomet to go to the mountain.

It is unlikely that any will deny the existence of a widespread desire for intellectual food, for mental acquisition and progress. The Chautauqua movement is evidence enough of this if evidence be called for. Nor can we doubt that many whose cravings for recreative occupation are now satisfied by the lightest of frivolities and the most unsubstantial of literary pabulum, may, by the right kind of effort, be stimulated to a higher intellectual life. These conditions are found widespread. Do they not exist among us today? The people then need leaders—those who shall tell them how to attain what they seek. Where shall they more fittingly look for such leaders than among the faculties of our Colleges and Universities?

The leading feature of the extension movement is the Extension Lecture Course. In any community where there is a sufficient number of persons desiring to take up the study of any subject, a suitable organization is formed to perfect and carry out the necessary arrangements. A capable instructor is secured. Tickets are sold at the lowest possible rate, for it is the aim to bring the opportunities of the course within the reach of the largest number. The lectures will occur at such intervals and be of such number as may suit each particular case. Among the ticket holders will be some who are content with simply listening to the lecturers, doing little or no supplementary studying. Others will wish to do somewhat thorough work upon the subject taken up. For the especial help of this latter class, a printed syllabus of the course is prepared and put into the hands of each person. This syllabus, besides giving an outline of the lectures, contains a list of books desirable for reference, and minute directions for study. Either before or after each lecture, the instructor meets those who wish to be considered as students, for an hour of recitation and discussion upon the lecture of the preceding week. At each such meeting, special work is assigned to individuals, to be written out and submitted to the instructor for criticism. Finally, after the completion of the course, an examination is offered to all who choose to take it, and certificates are given to those who reach a designated standard.

The general plan thus is very simple. Details will be modified to suit the circumstances of the lecturer or community. Extension Libraries of reference books may be provided and rendered accessible to students under proper regulations, with little individual expense. The syllabus, the private class, the special work submitted to lecturer for criticism, and the examination at the close of the course, are essential features of the extension lecture system. These are adapted to secure definite and permanent results, such as the mere listening to lectures cannot produce.

The beneficial effects of all this upon any community are seen at once. The Chautauqua Circles are doing much in the same line. But University Extension reaches out to a far larger number and brings with it the immense stimulus of personal contact with one who should be himself full of zeal and enthusiasm for that which he represents. From the standpoint of the College the advantage is equal. The personal mingling of the individual members of the faculty with the larger constituency of the institution, secures among the public a better and more general acquaintance with the institution; and if they be men worthy of respect and confidence, their influence will be very great. The institution will gain also in the number of those who come within its walls, through the awakening of dormant faculties which will call for larger opportunities. The instructor himself will be stimulated by the necessity of approving himself to the popular audience, and will in almost every case gain in clearness of thought, in ability to present his theme and to rouse absorbing interest in it. There is a danger to be guarded against— the temptation to make this popular work superficial and "catchy" rather than to rely on the intrinsic merits of the subject thoroughly treated, yet this danger being foreseen may be avoided.

A few practical suggestions: The value to a College of having its instructors appear before the public upon the lecture platform, take part in associations and conventions, has been pretty generally recognized. Such engagements however, as a rule, have been in addition to the regular and full work of the class-room, and have been merely private arrangements on the part of the instructors. Let this be changed. Let the Extension Department become an integral part of the college. Let the fees for the various courses conducted be paid into the college treasury. Let the class-room work required of the instructor be so diminished in amount, that he will be able, without additional expenditure of effort, to carry the Extension work. This change will make necessary an increase of college faculty, and in connection with this increase will naturally follow the advantage of increased specialization of work by the individual members of the faculty. The additional fees received will furnish at least a large part of the funds for carrying out the plan. Should they fail to suffice, I imagine that there are few departments of college work for which an adequate endowment will be more readily obtained.

No college can inaugurate such an undertaking without the very best of thoughtful and systematic effort. The co-operation of leading men in different localities must be secured. Especially must the pastors be brought to realize the value to their own work of the proposed plans. The beginnings will probably be small. There will undoubtedly be many disappointments and discouragements. But if energy and wisdom be used, what reasons are there why great results may not be reached? And perhaps sooner and more easily than anticipated. And why should not the College Extension Department become a bureau of information and assistance for all the college's constituency, aiding in arrangements for lectures other than those of regular Extension Courses, and for various entertainments of a character associated with the College work; advising Chautauqua Circles, Young People's Societies, and Literary Clubs in matters where such advice may be a help, and finding in the course of time many unforeseen methods of useful activity? Why may not the College often times prove a valuable helper to academies and schools with which it is intimately connected by allowing them the temporary service of its instructors in branches which especially demand to be taught by specialists? Why may not the College be the center of various clubs of cultured men and women, students in Biblical Literature, Science, Sociology and other lines of thought? Why, in a word, may not the College go out far more than it has done heretofore, among the people of the community, to stimulate them and help them amid the routine of daily tasks and duties, into a higher intellectual and spiritual life? Is not this possible?

THE IMPORTANCE OF A RELIGIOUS ATMOSPHERE IN OUR INSTITUTIONS OF LEARNING.

Rev. Geo. A. Rawson, Vernondale.

In order to fulfill their true mission, our Educational Institutions should seek to reach, develop and direct the whole circle of powers found in those who come under their influence and training.

The end aimed at should be a well-rounded manhood. They have to deal, very largely, with the raw material of human character. They take our young people at the formative, and so the most critical, period in their development; the period when they are the most open and the most sensitive to surrounding influences; and when they are eagerly and anxiously looking to their teachers and leaders to give them the key note, and to furnish them the pattern after which they shall fashion their own thought, and purpose and life.

If the only object of an education was to fit a man or woman for business proficiency, or for material advantage and success, then the moral and religious considerations might be left for others to look after, and our Institutions be given up wholly to the intellectual and secular training of our young people. This neglect, however, would be fatal to the highest good, and the noblest interests of those who are seeking to equip themselves for life's work. In a world where the forces of evil are so manifold and so great, it is essential to the safety and true success of those who are preparing themselves to meet these powers, and to accomplish the highest service, that they be securely anchored by an intelligent faith in Almighty God, and carry within them a pervading sense of their responsibility to Him.

An Institution is defective in its most vital point, and neglectful of its highest duty to God, to its students, and to society in general, when it ignores the moral and spiritual training of those who are to go out from its walls to become leaders of men in the various professions and walks of life. A collegiate course of training, undoubtedly, adds to a man's powers; he becomes more efficient as a worker for good, or as a worker for evil. The religious atmosphere of an Institution has more influence upon the development of character, than we, at first thought, may suppose. There are churches and communities where the atmosphere is so charged with spiritual influences as to be consciously and quickly felt by those who come within their circle. The same is true of certain Institutions of learning—may this become preeminently true of our Pomona College. In these Institutions it seems almost impossible for a young man or woman to remain very long without becoming deeply impressed, and being drawn into the current of its religious life.

We know how powerfully the intangible thing called air, or atmosphere affects us; how it may carry upon its invisible wings, depression, weakness, disease and death; or it may become a minister of life, imparting health, vigor and tonic to all our vital forces. There is such a thing as an intangible religious, or spiritual atmosphere— an atmosphere that penetrates the innermost life of the man, bringing wonderful quickening, health, vigor, to the moral and spiritual forces within. It is the breath of God; it comes to us from the pure mountain tops, where rests the sunlight of heaven. How is it to be brought down into this lower sphere, brought down and made to pervade the halls of our Institutions, where our young people are congregated, and where they are awakening to a consciousness of life, and the vital powers within them are being stirred into unwonted activity. Not by the mere perfunctory teaching of religious truth, nor the mere mechanical grinding out of religious exercises. The atmosphere of such cold, religious formalism, is charged with double skepticism and spiritual death.

These young people are full of life; a religion to have influence with them must have life in it. That life is born of a vital faith in God, of a reverent regard for His word, and of a pervading love for the souls of the young, on the part of those who fill the chairs, and are the appointed leaders in these Institutions. Men thus embraced with the love of God and the spirit of Christ, will create an atmosphere around them, saturated with moral and religious life.

Let these Colleges and Schools be enthroned in the prayers of the churches, and in the prayers of the homes from which the young are gathered, and we shall see a stalwart, manly procession of young men coming forth from them to do a grand work for God and humanity.

THE WORKMAN HIS OWN BEST TOOL.
Rev. Henry W. Jones, Pasadena.

I am to show up an error which it is the mission of the Christian College to correct, an error which has invaded our American civilization, must we not confess temporarily mastered it? It is respecting the true place and power of money.

A turning away from other modes of securing ones ends to the use of money in attaining them.

The end in view is power, that ability to do anything and everything which money is supposed to possess. I will not deny that it has a large degree of the efficiency that is attributed to it. In the present state of society the general estimate is at least somewhere near the truth. But let us know what this error is doing for us in certain directions.

Trace its effects in trades, manufacture and even professions. It says whatever adaptabilities I may have for this business I will disregard, except as they indicate somewhat how I can get rich the fastest. The particular calling I follow will be for the sake of the money I can make in it. With that I am to make my impression on the world. Thus one's calling becomes incidental, transitional, to be abandoned for anything else that pays better. Will he now be likely to chose it as carefully or learn it as thoroughly? Take the medical profession. Certainly here the mischief of the commercial spirit is evident. They, to whom we so intrust our lives as to physicians, ought to be as thoroughly prepared for the great responsibility as study and entire devotion to their calling can make them. But there are many who enter it merely to make money, to leave it for something else, if it should disappoint this expectation. What incentive is there to thoroughness in preparation for a career so uncertain? "For men who take the first rank, or even the second, in the professions," as another truly says, "there may and ought to be large pecuniary rewards. But these emoluments are never legitimately more than incidents of the calling. If money is set up as the highest ideal and aim, the chances are that the individual will become a mere grubber, or one of hopeless professional mediocrity."

This commercial spirit appears in our politics. It is not an accident that the United States Senate is gradually becoming a body of millionaires. Is it true that to secure a fortune is the way to obtain the highest offices in state and nation? Is it true on the other hand that to secure office is the shortest way to a fortune? What does the fact prophesy for the future of our Republic that year by year a larger number of votes are purchasable, and that business men prefer to contribute money for political purposes rather than to give personal attention to political duties even so much as to vote? A leading business man of New York confessed for himself and his class, "We have thought this thing over, and we find that it pays better to neglect our city affairs than to attend to them; that we can make more money in the time required for the full discharge of our political duties than the politicians can steal from us on account of our not discharging them." It is needless to ask what sort of government will result from that style of citizenship.

See what this spirit is doing in the sphere of journalism. The function of the newspaper is to give the news, reports of actual occurrences from day to day, with due regard to their intrinsic importance, to the public morality and to personal rights. Whether the actual newspaper fulfills this ideal I need not ask. If not, complaint is silenced, and that satisfactorily to most minds, when it is said for the publisher that he runs his press to make money. What else does he do it for? In the editorial columns, the editor is supposed to be giving his own opinions, and to be contending for his own principles. Is he doing this today? Hear what he is reported to have said in a speech at a press dinner in New York lately: "I am paid $150 per week for keeping honest opinions out of the paper I am connected with. Others of you are paid similar salaries for doing similar things. If I should allow honest opinions to be printed in one issue of my paper, like Othello, my occupation would be gone. The business of a leading journalist is to distort the truth, to vilify, to fawn at the feet of Mammon, and to sell his country and his race for daily bread, or for what is about the same, his salary. You know this, and I know it, and what foolery to be toasting an independent press. We are the tools and vassals of rich men behind the scenes. We are jumping jacks. They pull the string and we dance. Our time, our talent, our possibilities are all the property of other men. We are intellectual prostitutes." Let us call this an exaggeration; there is truth enough in it to show that this profession has not escaped the contagion of the commercial spirit.

Again. This error would revolutionize our system of education. The true object of what we call education is not to fit one out with trade or profession. When it has done its work it has made a man or woman, not a joiner, or a doctor, or a merchant, or a school teacher. At a particular time he will begin to learn his trade or profession, but that is not in any true sense his education. One might almost say that his education leaves off at the point where his trade training or profession training begins. Now this false idea respecting money makes the chief question in education. "What studies will pay best?" And it goes on to ask, "Latin? Who ever saw a bank check written in Latin? Greek? The idea that a man can't secure a lucrative practice as a physician unless he can read Thucydides. Do a tailor's suits bring any higher prices, or does he get any more to make for his familiarity with Aristotle or Dugald Stuart?" Yet how many parents make a fatal mistake here! Said President Gates, of Amherst College, lately, "What right has any father whose circumstances are such as to make it possible to give his son a liberal education—what right has any such father to shut his son forever out from those broad horizons of life which belong to the liberally educated man? When the son, who is to you as the apple of your eye, stands before you in his early teens, let the arch enemy of all goodness offer you any prize he will on condition that you will bind forever to his side that son's right arm. Suppose that by thus maiming and disfiguring God's likeness in his body you could start him in life with more money at thirty years than he could hope to attain in any other way. Would the prospect for a moment tempt you? And is it a less serious matter to dwarf the soul and cripple the divine energies of the mind and heart? You would reject with indignant scorn the offer of a fortune won by allowing him to be physically maimed; and can we who are able to send our sons on into the larger life which only prolonged education can procure for them, for a moment tamper with the question whether some added keenness in money getting, and the somewhat earlier attainment of the means of self-support, should be held a good and sufficient reason for the eternal dwarfing of the mind and soul of the sons whom God has intrusted to our care?"

This error turns aside many a young man fitted for a high position in the ranks of usefulness, where he is greatly needed. "There are more ways than one of doing good," he says. What is so powerful an influence as money? Once I get fairly at work with my talents. and I can support half a dozen missionaries." But the half a dozen embryo missionaries that he would be willing to support hear his reasoning about money, follow his example, and each of them sets about raising money enough to support half a dozen missionaries. Many a man of those best fitted for personal work in the spheres of religion and benevolence excuses himself. "I can't spare time and thought for such things," he says. A man to succeed in business must devote his whole energies to it. Accordingly this one thing I do. I will earn and others will do the personal work. Let the ministers do it. Hire some one from the Young Men's Christian Association. It is not in my line. Every man to his trade." And unless his principles are wrong he is right. A gentleman, trained to business, said to another, who was in need of a partner, "I have been long intimate with the business men of this city; can I not meet your want?" "You'll excuse me, but you have the reputation of being interested in matters outside of business." "Yes, and I trust I shall always deserve that reputation." "Oh, but you know that business, as it is now conducted, is a bit of rope with a man at each end, toe to toe, and if either slacks up, ever so little, the other jerks it away." "Yes, I know it; it is a true picture drawn to life." "You see? You'll excuse me." And he bowed him out. I need not ask whether these promises of financial aid to philanthropical enterprises are generally fulfilled, which men make to their better nature when they thus substitute their earnings for their personal service. If they are, then the treasuries of churches, colleges, benevolent societies, hospitals, etc., are full. "Yet," as another says, "the truest and best help anyone can give to others is not in material things, but in ways that can make them stronger and better. Money is good alms when money is really needed; but in the divine gift of hope, friendship, courage, sympathy, and love, it is paltry and poor. Usually the help people need is not so much the lightening of their burdens as fresh strength to enable them to bear their burden and stand up under it. The best thing we can do for another, some one has said, is not to make some things easy for him, but to make something of him."

How unfavorable to personal culture is this commercial atmosphere. How many drop music, standard literature, art study and practice, elocution, debate, one thing or another in which they might have excelled, to the delighting and instructing of the circle of near friends and often of a wider public. It blights the shoots of originality and tends to reduce society to monotony, as well as mediocrity.

Under this regime the comfort of life languishes. These whom we are contemplating are Mammon's martyrs. Talk of the privations of missionaries. Here are multitudes of people enduring worse privations in the sight of plenty, with no consciousness of nobleness to sustain them, no outlook on ripening fields of usefulness around them which their own hands have sown, no smile beaming on them of admiring angels, watching them with the earnest sympathy of colaborers. And they never will enjoy life, these martyrs who have turned their crowns into money. To extract pleasure from money is an art, requires study, practice, like any art. When their set time comes to turn their money into pleasure they will have no idea how to do it, any more than the boy who spent his first $5 for honey and sat down before it for the best good time he ever had in his life.

Have you heard of the discovery of the philosophers' stone? If not, what is it then that is turning everything into gold? The toilful search for it, of which we have read, was always with the pleasantest anticipations of what was to be done with the gold into which everything would be turned. Was there then no anxious inquiry what was to be done without the things which were to be thus transmuted. Alas, there is none. It is easy, in picturing what things money can do, to forget what good things it can undo. It is an enemy not to be surrendered to without debasement.

Thou shalt lower to his level day by day,
What is fine within thee growing coarse to sympathize with clay.
* * * * * * Thou art mated to a clown,
And the grossness of his nature will have weight to drag thee down."

Money is not that one tool of our earthly calling, to buy which we can afford to sell all our other faculties and endowments. The Christian College stands as a living protest against this error, teaching that our one great implement is ourselves; our one great work, usefulness. As the united testimony of its various departments, to its students, and through them in the world it says:

Life should mean, first, self-development. We ought to find our greatest self-satisfaction in seeing our own faculties grow and expand. The skill that can make an invisible joint in a piece of furniture, or a smoothly working piece of delicate machinery in brass or iron; the ability to draw a graceful outline, to lay forms and colors together so as to rival nature's landscapes, to write or execute music that can make the very soul march or halt; these are the possibilities which God has planted in us. Shall they be suffered to die out? Shall the hills and valleys of our varying individualities be graded off by this money-making propensity and society reduced to a dead level that has no outlook beyond dollars and cents? Of two things which a man can do well he ought to choose for his calling the nobler. If we can bless the world directly with voice, pen or skillful hand-labor as much as by turning our labor into money, the former is the nobler life, the life for us.

For, life should mean, secondly, usefulness. Ourselves, our sympathy, our voices, the deeds of our hands, work that has personality in it, are immeasurably more potent for good than the money into which we are too glad to transmute these. To make something and sell it, and with the proceeds hire some one to go and visit a sick family, is a very roundabout way of relieving their wants. For some unfortunate people, to be sure, it is the only method available. Alas, that any should prefer that way. Always our study should be, how can myself be most useful? By no proper use of terms can I call my money myself! When an opportunity is offered to serve mankind directly with my hands, my feet, my voice, my loving sympathy, my prayers, I make a sad bargain, if I sell myself and hand over the price.

> "Not what we give but what we share,
> For the gift without the giver is bare;
> Who gives himself with his alms, feeds three,
> Himself, his hungering neighbor, and Me."

CHRISTIAN EDUCATION.

Stephen Bowers, A. M., Ph. D.

Herbert Spencer says that the function that education has to discharge is to prepare us for complete living. Under this beautiful mask, however, is hidden the most complete agnosticism. Mr. Spencer nowhere, in defining education, gives us the remotest hint that man has a religious nature to be educated. Follow him through his definitions and the thirsty soul will find no place of refuge, no resting place. Someone has said: "His complete living appears in the light of all history exceedingly incomplete." The fact is, his theories of education have the qualities of but half truths. They do not reach Christian consciousness. The Christian theory of education is implied in the Christian conception of human life, and we must learn from Christ what complete living is.

I cannot do better in this connection than to quote a brief paragraph from a recent writer: "Education, says he, should be in the largest sense liberal. It should make the man self-supporting, acquainting him with practical measures for comfortable and beautiful living. It should prepare him for citizenship. It should make him, it may be, a man of letters, or a scientist, or an artist. But it should go further. It should strengthen and broaden his faith in God. It should sharpen his appreciation for spiritual realities. It should furnish him with a just conception of human life; its needs, possibilities and obligations. It should deepen in his mind the distinction between right and wrong. It should strengthen his convitcion of those truths which surround right with its most impressive sanctions."

Now I submit that any system of education that does not accomplish this is a failure. It will leave the student but half educated. If he is in some sense fitted for living here, he is not for the great hereafter. The theory that banishes all religious instruction from the public school is narrow and incomplete. It is a concession to skepticism, and is as irrational as to concede the demands of the drunkard-maker who would banish all books on the evils of intemperance.

Christianity is the great underlying principle upon which this government is founded. It is the corner stone, the foundation rock, upon which the national fabric is constructed. Remove this and the building will fall into decay. In order to instill patriotism into the heart of the child, the State displays the national banner over the school house and recommends text-books that tell of the heroic deeds of our fathers. This should also apply to Christian principle if we expect our children to become Christians, patriots, and law abiding citizens.

A dozen years ago the public schools in my town were closed on the occasion of horse races, that teachers and children might witness the elevating pastime.

One might as well look for the healthy growth of a tree after its roots have decayed, as to expect vigorous moral growth from schools where moral precepts and principles are ignored. And what will the end be? I will let Jules Simon, in an article on public education in France in the *Contemporary Review*, answer the question. He says: " In the olden time we used to have in the school those little books of sacred history which opened with the words: 'In the beginning God created the heaven and the earth.' We have done away with these little books now. The children will hear no more talk of creation or of God, or even of a beginning. In one word, the school they will have to learn in will be strictly neutral. This is what they tell us by way of consolation. *They forget that it is not God we are afraid of, it is Nihilism.*"

It would be well for us in America to take the hint. This unrest and tendency to Nihilism is cause for alarm. Left to themselves, men tend to anarchism, nihilism and other baneful isms. Christian education is the antidote. Let us be less afraid of the great and loving God, and more afraid of violating his divine laws.

When a generation is raised up in this country without faith and without respect for Christianity, our decadence as a nation begins. Let not the era predicted by Carlyle come to this land, "when he that is least educated will chiefly have it to say, he is least perverted."

Our most enlightened people see the necessity of Christian education and the thorough Christianizing of our secular colleges and universities.

I contend that one of the chief requisites of college education is thorough and systematic Christian education. I do not wish to be understood as desiring our Colleges and Universities to be turned into Theological schools. Far from it. But were I a teacher, instead of an editor, I think I would make a specialty of the history of Christianity, and endeavor to show what impression it has made upon the opinions of mankind; how it has affected civilization, and the countries of the world. This, with its phenomenal extension makes up one of the most interesting, and at the same time the most important chapter in the world's history. I would endeavor to show that:

> "In all our way through life it sheds
>   Its bright and healing beams
>   O'er all our woes.
>   And when our days are done
>   It lights the path to brighter
>   Happier scenes.
>   And it will live and shine when
>   All beside has perished
>   In the wreck of earthly things."

I would endeavor to remove doubts from the minds of the people. The struggle with doubt often begins in college days. There seems to come a time in the life of every boy when, in his imagination, he has advanced beyond the knowledge of parent and teacher. That is the hour frought with greatest danger, and one that appeals to the wise teacher for assistance.

Let the *science* of Christianity be taught; its rules, its principles, its ethics. This in a sense implies that inner experience, so essential on the part of the minister and teacher—personal contact and communion with God through his Son. The student must be taught to realize that the highest Christian knowledge is not attainable in the study of books, but by Christian living; and that the best ritualism is in doing the just and the generous, the merciful and the Christ-like.

Now, brethren, the practical question for us to consider is the importance of planning liberal things for the endowment of the schools in our midst, and especially that one known as Pomona College.

While other speakers will doubtless have suggestions to make concerning this matter, I may be allowed to say that in my humble opinion its success lies within the reach of the pastors of Southern California. I base this upon experience in other places, and observation as to other churches. In a letter from the President I was impressed with the words: "We must aim high and determine that no student shall suffer intellectually by taking his course of study in a Christian College." I do not wish to lay on ministers of Christ additional burdens, or emphasize those already upon them, but in their hands rest possibilities for its endowment that will lift this noble young institution above want. What class of men is so well prepared to grapple with a problem like this? They themselves are educators and moulders of public sentiment.

This may be done by educational sermons in which the wants of the school, its aims, its purposes, its possibilities for good for the upbuilding of young men and young women, and shaping their course into lives of usefulness may be made prominent. It may also be done by seeking bequests, donations and subscriptions from men and women whom God has blest with wealth. Let every pastor study its needs, and the grand and far-reaching possibilities in Christian propagandism and soul saving until his heart is thrilled and set on fire, and he will be prepared to present them to others. This cannot be done in a perfunctory or half-hearted way. It must be done with an earnestness begotten of love to God and love to man. This generation is laying the foundation for still greater things in the next. If the wheels of Christianity and civilization continue to move forward, education a century hence will be far in advance of what it is now. Then let the foundation be laid wide and deep, and let us build for all time.

I would have our Colleges and Universities manned with Christian teachers—teachers who fear God and work righteousness; for I can think of few more responsible places in which one can be placed than that of instructor of youth. To shape the destiny of minds that are to live when this world's entire history will be but a leaf in the book of eternity.

> "We should be wary, then, who go before
> A myriad yet to be; and we should take
> Our bearings carefully, where breakers roar,
> And fearful tempests gather, for one mistake
> May wreck unnumbered barks that follow in our wake."

CHRISTIAN EDUCATION AND MUSIC.

Professor A. D. Bissell, Saticoy.

The place accorded to music in Christian education will depend on the place we allow it in Christian life. I feel under obligations to the first speaker before this Convention for the admirable analysis of mental activity he presented, making it easy to show what place music may have in Christian life. In the arch of mental activity, the emotions, said the speaker, constitute the keystone. The case may be more strongly stated by saying with Lotze that the emotions are the root out of which grow the twin trunks of knowledge and will. There are deep recesses of the soul into which the scalpel of consciousness cannot penetrate for dissection. But, though closed to analysis, inmost souls have wide avenues of approach for the reception of impressions from various sources; and here chiefly is the sphere of art as a power in life, whether literary, plastic or musical. There are these three forms of art, and the greatest of these is music. That is, music is capable of influencing a larger number more forcibly than either of the others. The province of music in Christian life is then:

Firstly, to beget and strengthen Christian emotion, and out of Christian emotion and impulse grows Christian action and character. Men who have no special interest in Christian ideas and worship will attend public service and even sing in choirs out of love for music, and many are the cases of men who got their first vital contact with Christian ideas through the service of song.

Secondly, to serve as a vehicle or medium for the expression of Christian emotion, and more especially the emotions that pass like electric shocks from man to man in an audience. We are undemonstrative and often feel the need of a vent for overfull hearts. To refer to my own experience; I listened not long ago to a sermon that moved me deeply, but how deeply I did not realize until in singing the closing hymn, "Bethany," the feelings that had been stirred within me came to a head and burst forth in song, while I longed as never before in my life to be brought nearer to God even by my woes. And no sermon ever gave me such a might of conviction, fortified by emotion, as that wonderful chorus in Handel's immortal

Oratorio of the Messiah, where orchestra, organ and chorus join in crashing chords, "His name shall be called Wonderful! Counselor! The Mighty God! The Everlasting Father! The Prince of Peace!"

My plea is for more attention to the cultivation of the voice in singing. The tendency is now toward instrumental music, and development of technical dexterity is far more in demand than soulful expression of deep feeling. There is a great neglect of singing; witness the congregational singing in our churches. On all sides I hear the complaint, "We have a large number of nice young people, but they don't know how to sing." But neglect of singing means decline of music as a fine art. For the inward appreciation and love of music is the essence of the art, and nothing gives such an appreciation and sense of the power and beauty of music as the ability to share in producing it. A man may arrive at an intellectual understanding of a Bethoven Symphomy by a careful study of the score; but give the same man a violin or other instrument and put him in the orchestra, and the same composition has a new meaning and beauty. The mere pleasurable admiration of mechanical dexterity or enjoyment of sweet sensations of sound have little or no value for the inner life, and are of use only as a lever to lift the student to a higher plane. But the ability to sing, to feel oneself borne up in common with others on pinions of song, can be a mighty instrument for good in Christian and church life. Can we secure good singing?

Some teachers go so far as to say that any one who can talk can be taught to sing. I would prefer to put it this way; any one who has ear enough to distinguish between the falling inflection of a positive assertion and the rising inflection of a question has ear enough to learn to sing. If you don't believe it, come and try me. I might find considerable difficulty with some hard cases, but if children are taken sufficiently early the hard cases would be reduced to a minimum.

How many ministers find their work hampered, themselves fettered, because they cannot lead their congregations in giving vent to their feelings in a song of penitence, of confession, gratitude, praise, communion with Christ, and consecration to his service! But when a man goes into a Christian College he may be already so fixed in the habit of not singing that he cannot be trained, except at disproportionate expense and trouble. The time and place to begin cultivating the voice and musical taste is in childhood and in the home or graded school. Then as students come to the College the finishing touches can be added, independence acquired, and each student equipped with a powerful instrument. Training to high technical development, to intelligent appreciation of the highest forms of art, is not a necessary part of Christian education, much as I would like to see such work more widely spread than it now is. But training to participate with others in the various possible functions of music in Christian life, to distinguish between good music and trash, this can be well-nigh universal, and ought to have a large place in any scheme of education that claims to be liberal and Christian.

THE TRANSFORMING POWER OF COLLEGE LIFE.

Rev. Francis M. Price, Bethlehem, Los Angeles.

In the city of Tai-ku, China, standing amid the many haunts of idolatry, is a grand old Confucian temple, which, with its various out-buildings, covers an area of about five acres; and although having suffered much from the dilapidations of time it is still the admiration and pride of the city. It is a temple devoted to learning. Over the great gateway, through which all who enter its hallowed precincts must pass, is a motto in four, large, gilded Chinese characters, with this sentiment: "Doctrine Crowns the Ages," the meaning of which is that the teaching of the great Confucius is the glory of the past and present. For China, no words could be truer. They express the sentiment of every Chinaman. His system is best studied in his "Great Learning," which is a brief essay of 205 words, claims to be the "gateway of virtue," and has no less an object than the "pacification of the whole world."

In this he says: "The ancients"—and with the Chinese all good things come from the ancients—"wishing to make virtue illustrious, first governed well their own kingdoms; wishing to govern their own kingdoms well, they first ruled well their own families; wishing to rule well their own families, they first regulated their own bodies; wishing to regulate their own bodies, they first rectified their hearts; wishing to rectify their own hearts, they first purified their motives; wishing to purify their motives they first perfected their knowledge and the perfection of knowledge is found in a study of the nature of things."

Thus by adjusting individual lives according to the nature of things, he hoped to reach the grand object of pacifying the whole world. No heathen ethical system approaches it in grandeur and simplicity, and yet, noble and comprehensive as it is, it fails to take in the true nature and destiny of men; and however elaborately the details of his system may be worked out, it can never be complete; it offends at a crucial point.

His was the great arch with every stone highly polished and fitted in with great exactness, but it lacked the key-stone. Later in the development of this system a wise commentator saw this defect and expressed the belief that a great teacher would come from the West to "complete the system." We, of the West, believe that we have found the keystone to this arch, and we express our convictions by prefixing to our educational systems the noble word "Christian." A Christian education, a Christian College, is the crowning glory of the present age, the fairest flower that grows in the soil of the church, promising the richest fruit. The object of the Confucian system was exhaustively to cultivate; the object of the Christian system is to cultivate and transform—not simply scholarship, but scholarship controlled and glorified by Christian character.

But wherein lies the power to secure this crowning excellence? In what part of the curriculum or college life shall we find it? I answer, it lies largely in the *esprit de corps* of the institution, and this must lie first of all in the College faculty. The motto of the teacher soon becomes the motto of the pupil. Let us have no heathen or worldly-wise mottoes written over our college gateways such as: "Learning crowns the ages," "Know thyself," "Knowledge is power," "Success crowns the diligent," or "There is room at the top." But let us write in letters of gold over our gateways, in our halls and recitation rooms, the motto of the "Great-heart of our Congregational Churches"—the sainted Dr. Goodell—who lived as truly as he said: "There is nothing worth living for save the glory of Christ." It is not simply the principles of morality and good character that we want but *enthusiasm for our glorious and glorified Master.* Nothing less than this will suffice; nothing less than this is worthy of our Christian College. It is not minds well trained, but minds set on fire with enthusiasm for our Redeemer's cause. Enthusiasm in an untrained mind often runs into fanaticism; but true enthusiasm, born of the Spirit of God, held in control by a trained head and heart, is the greatest power in this world.

Count von Zinzendorf, the founder of the sect of the Moravian Brethren, a people whose devotion to the Master is known in every part of the world, imparted such enthusiasm to the brethren of that sect as to make them wellnigh invincible in every undertaking. The secret of his success lay in the motto of his life—"Ich habe eine passion, est ist er nur er;" I have one passion, it is He only He."

The Christian Church began in a white heat of enthusiasm for the Master—an impulse from the mighty Spirit of God. Then men rejoiced that they were counted worthy to suffer for His name and sold their farms and gave the money to the church; now many who confess Christ count it a great cross to suffer for his sake and rob the church of its dues to buy a farm. Our church life must be filled and thrilled with enthusiasm for our Master before it can hope to conquer this money-seeking, pleasure-loving world. We must look to our Colleges and Seminaries to give the church leaders, whose enthusiasm will be contagious, last from January 1st to December 31st, from taking up of the cross, until the time when they shall receive their crown.

There is one scene of my college life that I shall never forget. It was near the close of the senior year, and the class had gathered for a special meeting before graduation. The president, some of the professors, and the pastors of the two churches were present. Brief, incisive, and impressive addresses were made in which the Master's claims were set forth with great simplicity, and the quiet though powerful spiritual influence was well nigh irresistible. It was the culmination of the spiritual influences that had been thrown around that class for four years. At last it was proposed that President Fairchild close with prayer for all who desired to be especially remembered. One after another presented brief requests and among others a man who had resisted every influence through his course of study, and was going out from the College an infidel, arose and requested prayers. A wave of deep emotion passed over the assembly. Every head was bowed and almost every eye was filled with tears, for I believe he was the only unconverted man in his class.

Oh, it is a great thing to bring young men and women face to face with God and duty when they are deciding the question of a life work, for only thus can the right decision be made.

Young men and women carry with them through life the spirit of the institution in which they receive their higher education. It is something that they cannot escape even if they will, and ordinarily the brighter the student the more thoroughly he is possessed of this spirit. The subtle, potent *esprit de corps* of the College life speaks persuasively to the young people under its influence, and with cumulative power as the years pass. "Be ye transformed into my image," and if Christ be the sum and substance of this College enthusiasm, then the image into which they are transformed is the image of Christ.

THE KIND OF MEN DEMANDED OF THE CHRISTIAN COLLEGE.

PROF. C. S. NASH, PACIFIC THEOLOGICAL SEMINARY, OAKLAND.

The Christian College is responsible to Him whose name it bears. Subordinately and practically it must answer to His representatives on earth. The Christian Church, or any true portion of it, not only may but must hold the Christian College to account for its stewardship. If that stewardship has been faultily discharged, it may be partly because they who represent the Lord have not made His claims authoritative and irresistible. This paper would, therefore, be glad to engage attention both within and without College walls, hoping to serve humbly the discussion of our common duty.

1. In the first place, then, men of the best education are demanded of the Christian College. There must be excellence of result here. Failure cannot be excused. The Christian College must give its students as good a College training as they could find anywhere. It must send them out able to keep abreast of other College graduates. Or, better still, it must be able to give each man his utmost development. To this the College is held by various forces.

Competition is one of them. As for the Colleges which appear to be beyond the reach of this, the fact that they have the fields to themselves and the students in their power should make them even more solicitous to furnish the very best wares in the market. A Christian school is expected to avoid the unrighteousness of a railroad monopoly. Yet competition is at work even in such isolated regions. The world is small and open. The young man who discovers that the article offered at his door is second-rate will swing off tomorrow in search of the best until he find it. This compulsion is felt by a College through various channels. It comes through the students often. No institution can shake itself free from the intelligent judgment of its pupils. Whether appearing in criticism or in attempted revolution or in departure, that judgment is worthy of heed as the mouthpiece of maturer voices caught from a distance by alert ears. Again, parents and friends and the wider public wield the force of College competition. The practical and selfish world cares little to apply the righteous principle, "To each one according to his needs." It prefers the other righteous principle, which has a business look, "To him that hath shall be given." The ducats and the pupils go mainly to the Colleges that have the most of both.

In a higher way also the same call sounds in the ears of every institution. Above the din and strife of competition our schools meet as friends and helpers, imparting to one another, stimulating one another. Every high quality anywhere visible is a ringing challenge to the whole sisterhood. Each one that is alive feels the pull of this influence, just as a true man in the presence of another true man is kindled toward higher manhood. Again, there are Christian souls at large who, without a business threat, announce the divine desire to the College, cheering it on with courageous words, with gifts, with prayer. Its leaders also know how to draw near and catch the heavenly voice for themselves, as Elijah did at Sinai.

In the precise point, then, of its graduates, for which alone the College exists, we find the demand of God to be that they be made men of the best education. If they fall below this, God will use them according to their ability; but the missing portions of their development will He require at the hands of the College.

2. Again, men of Christian faith and character are demanded of the Christian College.

The whole attention of the College should not be absorbed in the educational line. Its name and assumed character bring forward the spiritual side of life. We believe it right to press the appeal that it send out Christian men. It is not enough that the College authorities rejoice, if by unusual and occasional methods God secure the conversion of students independently of their effort. Let the College that calls itself Christian legislate this element into its corporate life and its yearly plans. Then let the working force of the College carry out this design as zealously and faithfully as the curriculum of study. Let it no more strive to send out men of knowledge, of thinking habits, of speaking power, than it strives to send out men of Christian faith, hope, love, prayer and spiritual activity.

This demand is emphasized by important considerations. In the first place, College students are impressible. They are like clay in the hands of the potter. Few are quite mature and fixed. The great majority are present for the express purpose of being moulded and stamped. The character of many is determined forever in College. That of many others might be settled, probably that of nearly all. Our educators have the determination of immortal characters in the crisis of life, and too many of them forget the grandeur and gravity of their responsibility. College men can be won to Christ. There is no need of receiving so many back from the hands of the College spiritually unformed and deformed. College revivals have proven how grandly God can claim His own among these purposeful young lives. Again, conversions among College students are of the very best quality. Let no man say that the College course is no place for such matters. Results prove it to be the place of places. Prof. Henry Drummond declares, regarding Christians, that what is wanted is "not more of us, but a better brand of us." Now in the Colleges can the best brands be made. Conversions there are usually free from unbalanced emotion. The deep significance of the matter is appreciated, the elements of it are weighed, action is clear-sighted, deliberate, thorough. Christian character of the highest type and Christian activity of the noblest efficiency result from such conversions. Once more, Christian faith and character are the critical things of Christian education. Presumably there are many even Christian educators in our land who would claim that religion lies outside the schools. We are here today, however, to stand with those who maintain that the object of College training is nothing less than character. We do not want graduates with bodies and brains simply. We want purified hearts and renewed wills. We want all the pure, strong things of character, above all, the incomparable things found nowhere apart from personal experience of the power of Christ. Let our schools prepare us these. Let the Christian College at least acknowledge the demand and answer it according to its name. A College must bring forth men. A Christian College must bring forth Christian men.

3. In the third place, the demand on the Christian College is that the men and women of the best education and those of Christian faith and character be the same men and women. We cannot be satisfied that some should be trained intellectually and others spiritually. In that case we should be no whit in advance of the present conditions. The institutions that claim the greatest educational power often excuse themselves from spiritual responsibility. And they are apt to have poor respect for the sister schools which include the religious elements. We would challenge the implication that the highest scholarship and the best spirituality cannot thrive in the same College halls. They can live together even in one professorial chair, and can be built into young life synchronously

to their mutual advantage. We dare to say that a Christian civilization should build up an educational system, in which each separate school should bear the double character and do the double work; whose declared aim should be to graduate each pupil thoroughly educated and personally Christianized. If this be called intolerable coercion on the spiritual side, let it also be called so on the intellectual side, where it is being enforced stringently every day.

Now, to indicate practically for what such men and women are wanted, the following is offered. First, there is need of Christian scholars for the leading places in the educational world. The word *Christian* is here emphasized. *Christian* specialists are called for in every line of research, publication and instruction. Should the progress of a Christian civilization be led by ungodly men? Should the church act only when driven to it by foes, or when frightened into it by the direction of irreligious leaders? Should the advanced work of the age in language, in philosophy, in archæology, in natural science, in art, in political science, in sociology, in ethics even, be left to men whose enthusiasm and aim are purely of the earth? The church is under Divine commission to lead mankind, to do the foremost work, to uncover every item of hidden knowledge, to make it accessible to all men, to administer it for the present and eternal good of the race and for the glory of God. But in this matter the competitive law of life cannot be defied. The mighty men shall be they who are mighty. The field will belong to the unchristian just so far as the church fails to possess it by the sheer power of masterful ability. I conceive, then, that the Christian

Colleges are set to the momentous task of raising up Christian specialists of all sorts for the advanced posts of the world's activity and progress. They should be on the lookout constantly for most capable and promising youth, whom they can guide into a scholar's life; youth whose qualifications for such a life include a glowing personal Christianity.

Once more, there is need of educated Christians for all the walks of life. Here the word educated is emphasized. All through the social, business and professional world there is a lack of Christian men and women who were trained according to the best educational standards of the age, who can therefore hold their own and more alongside educated non-Christians. The practice of personal Christianity must be carried into the highest places. Christian scholarship and Christian effort must show that in Christ and His Gospel lies the only solution of the burning questions of human weal. Everywhere will superior men wield the power; therefore let superior men be made Christians and Christian men be made superior, which is the very genius and proposal of Christianity.

Particularly in the ministry are men of education sorely needed just now. It was shown recently that of the 580 students in our seven Congregational Theological Seminaries last year ('90-'91) over 220 had never been to College at all, while over fifty had pursued only a partial course. What are the professedly Christian Colleges doing? They can provide men for the ministry and God will hold them to account for it. There must be an educated ministry in our home churches, if educated lay Christians are to be led and educated non-Christians are to be won. And it has been demonstrated to our heart's content that the Christian kingdom cannot prevail in heathen lands in the hands of any but the mightiest men of war in Christendom. May God soon rouse the Christian Colleges to the duty of furnishing the full tale of educated clergymen and Christian specialists, and of sending forth the rest of its pupils as Christians, and as trained Christians, into the world's thought and action. What higher mission has God entrusted to any of the sons of men?

In closing let me state briefly two or three suggested points, deserving fuller treatment.

(*a*). The importance of the College pastor problem. The ministrations which are theorized into the office of College pastor should certainly be provided for in some way.

(*b*). The need of Christian scholars in the professorships of Christian Colleges. Such workers are indispensable to such work as above described.

(*c*). The necessity of the most generous financial equipment for the Christian College. Dr. McLean remarked the other day: "You can't make 90 cent men in a 10 cent Institution." Friends of the churches, this whole matter tumbles back upon you considerably. You call in vain for the best work from the Christian Colleges, because you do not make them the best appointed institutions. Too often, as compared with the policy of the world, the church expects its servants to make "bricks without straw." The Christian College will become all that its constituents enable it to become. When these say so, it can have the first scholars of the age in its chairs.

When the church declares that the educators of the young must be Christian men and women, such will presently be furnished, superlatively equipped; and then the Christian Colleges will neither venture nor desire to ask non-Christians to their faculties. When the church insists that its sons and daughters with all their getting shall get Christian faith and character, as the prime elements of Christian education, the Christian Colleges will put forth graduates who answer the demand. The power of God is with the Christian church. When she, having listened heavenward, speaks out on this subject of education, the schools will hear, the State will also hear; for "Vox populi Dei, vox Dei," "The voice of God's people is the voice of God."

PLATFORM OF THE EDUCATIONAL CONVENTION.

Adopted Thursday Evening, April 14th, 1892.

RESOLUTIONS.

Resolved, That we recognize in the constitution of the human mind the necessity of distinctively Christian education, and believe it our duty to build a Christian College in California as our tribute to Christian civilization.

Resolved, That we would for the present devote our efforts to the development of a College, properly so called, rather than a University; that we would provide instructors, material, equipment and courses of study for such grades of work, as good as can be offered anywhere; that we would insure a pervasive Christian influence through a moral and spiritual atmosphere created by Christian teachers and Christian pupils and that we therefore commend the policy which prefers quality to numbers, and excludes unworthy pupils.

Resolved, That as representatives of the Congregational churches of Southern California we approve the faith of the Board of Trustees of Pomona College in going forward in the face of financial depression to carry out the plan of a College of the highest grade, because we believe that every right plan is feasible, and that God himself will be with those who go forward in strong confidence in Him.

Resolved, That we heartily approve the sentiment that the personal character of the teacher is of the highest importance in education, and that we need for the Christian College men who will give their lives to their pupils, rather than to the private laboratory or to the dative case.

Resolved, That we approve of the demand for large room for the study of the Scriptures of the Old and New Testaments, and would hail with special pleasure an endowment which would give the whole time of one man to the Department of Biblical Literature.

Resolved, That our hearts unite in the prayer that out of Pomona College may come men whose work shall be as powerful as that of the College men who led the Reformation—men who will ally themselves with the righteous cause, however unpopular, and with the indomitable courage which knows no failure.

Resolved, That the Preparatory School of Pomona College should be made to be the best of its kind, but that no movement should be made to withdraw the children of Christian parents from the State High Schools, unless the influence of the teachers is known to be personally harmful.

Resolved, That the College Extension as presented to this Convention suggests to benefactors a most promising field for the use of funds, and we heartily commend it to the attention of Christian men and women of means as the best way to bring to all the churches the best influences of the College.

Resolved, That we heartily appreciate the offered aid of the American College and Education Society to pay toward the current expenses $4 to each $7 received upon the home field up to the sum of $4,000, and we respond to it by the recommendation that the Committee on Education appointed by our General Association prepare suitable blanks for a widespread subscription with the hope that the number of donors—in sums ranging from 25 cents to $100 each—may amount to 2,000, and that the average gift shall be $3.50, thus making up the grand total of $7,000, to which the College and Education Society will add $4,000. And that our children be invited to add their names thus to the roll of the builders of Pomona College.

Resolved, That the papers of this Convention be edited for early publication, and that a sufficient number of copies be placed for circulation in the hands of every pastor, to enable him to communicate to every family under his charge the force of their uplifting influence.

www.ingramcontent.com/pod-product-compliance
Lightning Source LLC
Chambersburg PA
CBHW030902170426
43193CB00009BA/712